BESTSELLING AUTHOR
KORIANNE MAR

PROPERTY: MASTER THE WEALTH

I0040014

The Ultimate Guide to
Create Financial Independence
and Wealth through
Smart Buy & Hold Cash
Flow Rental Property

Green Pinnacle

To YOU who will never stop searching for a better quality of life and more TIME to focus on things that matter

TABLE OF CONTENTS

Part 2: Process to Buy a Rental Property

Part 6: Building Your Financial Future

ACKNOWLEDGMENTS

Why did I start writing this book? I met my mentor before my summer vacation in 2015. He knew my personal life well and he asked me a few deep thought questions.

"What is next, Korianne? You have created financial independent and wealth, beautiful family life, outstanding health, you are living a fulfilled life with charity contributions. Can you help others to do the same?" he asked me. He said, "You do not want to die with your story, do you?"

After my last summer vacation with my boys, I decided to write this book. That was when I got started. I guess I do not want to die not sharing what I have learnt. Thank you to my mentor, GM, who gave me courage and who saw my gifts that can help others. My husband and my two sons are my reasons why I started the mortgage business and the real estate investment business. Thank you for your all unconditional love and unwavering support during my wide career ride. Thank you my niece, Mai, who adds more love and joy to our family and gives me an opportunity to support a daughter.

Thank you to my father, who instilled in me a lot of life values and taught me not to give up and to work hard on my dreams. Thank you my mother who taught me to be patient and took care of my sons while I was working long hours in the mortgage company and my real estate investment travels. Thank you all my sisters' family for their love, support, and laughter. Thank you Steve and Heather for their love and kindness to sponsor me live with them after I got out of refugee camp. Thank you, Kristi and Tristan for sharing your love and care to a big sister.

Thank you my two mentors, Albert and Mike, who transferred everything they know about the mortgage business and real estate investments so I was able to excel in both businesses. I wish you were both still around to see me today. RIP and I promise to share what I have learnt from you to better others' lives.

Thank you all the super real estate managers (Roger, Sarah, Steve, Patrick, Trish and Ron) who runs the business well for years. Some of you have been with me since I started the real estate investment business. You all give me TIME to focus on things that matter.

Thank you my business associates (Ken, Linh, Dave, Steve, Carl, Rich) that we often share our real estate strategies together and where to invest next.

INTRODUCTION

Have you ever noticed that when you are doing something you enjoy, time seems to fly by? Of course, when you have a job that you don't like, the time drags and you spend all of your time staring at the clock waiting for the day to end. I didn't want to spend my entire life watching a clock and hating work, so I decided to pursue a new career, something that I could actually enjoy.

I went into the rental business, and it has been my passion for more than fifteen years now. Being happy at work is something that I never thought I would experience. I've known so many people who disliked their job, and I'm grateful that I found a business that has allowed me to be financially independent, and that has the potential to create wealth for my family well into future generations.

I am so blessed and pleased to share the knowledge that I've gained with you, and I hope you employ my strategies to help you on your own path. It can help you to build your financial future, and many of you might find it to be a potential financial vehicle that you can use to build a business so you can finally quit that day job that has you sitting and staring at the clock.

Before we get into the details of using rental properties to create your wealth, I want to let you know more about me and the journey that brought me to this point. It's a long story, but I believe it serves to illustrate problems and concerns that many of you are probably facing right now.

What Was I Doing Before?

You might be wondering what type of job I had before I made the transition to be a real estate investor and buying rental properties.

Well, I was working in the high-tech industry for a few years before the last company I was working at shut down because they had no funding.

That is one of the dangers of working for someone else, especially in a field that has that sort of risk. You don't have control of what happens, and you might come into the office one day to find that the company you work for has been sold, or in my case, didn't have the funds to keep going.

It's scary.

Besides, I have witnessed a few family members who got laid off every few years. My brother-in-law, nephews, niece and husband went through a fewtimes job transitions.. When you work for a company, you really do not know what comes next, even if you try to prove yourself and put your hard work into it. It can happen to any of us when you work in a corporate job. Downsizing and layoffs are part of the normal cycle of maintaining a company running.

When I was out of work, I decided that there was no way I was going back into the corporate world. It wasn't something I enjoyed, and there was no future there for me. Let's go a little farther back in time, though, so you can get a better understanding of why I made the decisions that I did.

I thought back to the time when I worked for 3M. I had a little cubicle that I called "home" while I was at work. There were four co-workers who were seated in the same area, and they had an average of 20+ years of experience. In fact, one of them had been there for more than thirty years.

Even at that point, while at 3M, I would come home from work and think about what would happen to me if I were there for thirty years. Would I enjoy that type of life? My heart and my mind were both brutally honest with me and answered with a resounding "No."

Please don't misunderstand this. I know that sometimes you need to have those desk jobs. I'm someone who works hard, and it wasn't the work that was bothering me. It was the fact that I found the job to be extremely boring. Not only that, but when I looked at my bank account at the end of the month, I found that I couldn't put very much into my savings because I simply wasn't making enough.

When I realized that I wasn't bringing in enough money, I did the same thing that a lot of you probably do. I worked extra hard to show my worth to the manager. No matter how hard I worked, my annual raise was always the same – 8%. It was depressing, and I simply couldn't see myself sitting in that cubicle for another three decades just so I could get a pension.

So, I decided that I would leave 3M and look for another job. I received an offer that would provide me a 40% raise. It sounded great, and that was when I went to work for the high- tech company. You remember the one that shut down.

Nothing is certain. We can't have control over downsizing and layoffs when we are just worker bees. And that brings us back to the point where I decided that I would not get another corporate job.

What I Decided to Do

I was very fortunate that I had a husband who was very supportive of my decision to make a career change. We didn't have any children then, so I was able to take the time to figure what my passion was going to be. After about three months of searching, I settled on finance. I knew that I would enjoy it, since I liked working with numbers and I liked working with people.

At the time, I didn't know much about the field, so I decided to train. For three months, I trained extensively with a mortgage broker who had been in the business for more than thirty years and who was getting ready to retire. He taught me the ins and outs of the business, and after training, I got my license and opened up a mortgage company.

I was very excited that my business took off after about eight months, and I was able to earn a six-figure income. That's not to say that it all came easy, though. It was a lot of hard work and long hours that I spent learning to run and build a new business. I didn't mind the hard work, though, because I was determined not to go back into the unpredictable corporate world.

I was young and I knew that even if I made mistakes along the way, I could learn from them. I was just happy that I had found a business that I really did enjoy.

The First Rental and Beyond

Due to the success of my business, my husband and I were able to increase our savings and even buy a new house. We made sure it was in the best school district because we knew we wanted children down the road.

When we bought our new home, we didn't sell our old one. Instead, we became instant landlords by turning it into a rental. Even after all of the expenses were paid, we were able to see a positive cash flow of $500 a month. This was passive income, and I really liked the idea of that!

Next, I took a three-day real estate investment training course. This was in 2001, and I paid $7900 for the course. I felt it was well worth it, though, since it would provide me with more knowledge and more skill to advance a real estate business. I enjoyed the training enough that I decided to sign up for six months of private coaching.

While I was at the three-day seminar, I was lucky enough to have met a very knowledgeable builder. He was at the event with the goal of finding high net worth investors who would be interested in investing in his master senior community that would be going into Paradise Valley, Arizona.

At lunch, he presented his plan and said that he wanted to have $500,000 from each investor to join the senior community master plan. The plan involved building 100 homes, each of which would be in the $400k to $500k range.

I explained that we did not have $500k, and that we only had $200k in equity in the rental property we owned. I didn't have enough to invest in the project, but we did become friends afterwards. He was the one to advise me to sell the rental property and to use the equity to buy five more properties that would be able to generate $1500 a month rather than the $500 a month we were getting from the single rental that we had at the time.

I took his advice.

Let's look at the numbers so you can see how it all worked. They might seem a little confusing at first, but once you go through and read the rest of the book, everything will make more sense. For now, these can give you a good sense of how things can progress.

With the $230,000 in equity that we had, we were able to put 20% down on five new rental properties that we bought.

Purchase Price: $200,000
Down Payment: $40,000 (20%) + $6,000 (closing costs)
Loan Amount: $160,000 @ 6% (30-year fixed mortgage)

Rental Income: $2000
Mortgage Payment at 6% = $959
Tax = $300
Insurance = $100
Vacation Rate (5%) = $100
Maintenance (5%) = $100
Property mgmt. fee = $100

Total expenses = ($959 + $300 + $100 + $100 + $100 + $100) = $ 1659

Income: $2000
Expenses: $1659

Monthly Cash Flow: $341/month
Equity Pay Down: $159/month

Yearly Cash on Cash Return: $341 * 12 = $4,092/year

Annual Cash on Cash Yield: Annual cash flow/Total initial investment (Down payment + Closing cost)

Annual Cash on Cash Yield: $4092/$46000(down payment + closing cost) = 8.8%
This return does not count the equity payment of $159/month in the monthly mortgage payment.

From one property we had produced $500/month.
Now with *five* properties, each of them produced: $ 341 * 5 (rentals) = $1705/mo.

In 2001, from one rental sold we purchased five rentals.
In 2002, we purchased two more rentals from our savings.
In 2004 we refinanced our seven existing rentals and took money out.

Most of the properties were valued at $320,000 and we bought them for $200,000-220,000.

We were able to do a cash-out refinance for $53K for each property.

$300,000 * 80% = $240,000 (new loan amount)
$60,000 – $7,000 Refinance Cost = $53,000 cash back

$53,000 cash * 7 Properties = $371,000

Our initial capital: $230,000(2001) + $92,000(2002) = $292,000

Now we put $371,000 in our savings that we did not have to pay for capital gains tax. We again used this money to reinvest in other real estate rentals that produced monthly cash flow. In 2005 we bought ten more cash flow properties from a builder at 20% below market value. Four months later, we refinanced cash out to take our all the equity that we gained from these ten properties.

By the end of 2006, we owned twenty-eight rentals (single family, duplex, triplex, and fourplex) while I was still running a mortgage business.

I loved the mortgage business and helping my clients, but I had less interest because I worked long hours and missed a lot of quality time with my first son. I decided the mortgage business was not the right business for having a family. So, my career focus shifted to the rental business in 2008. Since then, profits from the rental business have exceeded that of my mortgage business.

From 2008 – 2011 I bought over forty projects from bank-owned, foreclosure properties, wholesale investors, and asset managers at deep discounts. I also fixed/flipped about a dozen projects, but found out the fixed/flipped strategy did not meet my financial objectives of return on investment for the amount of time and effort that I put in. But I did gain a great amount of knowledge with the flipping experiences and came to understand the price of materials much better that I could use to work with the property manager and contractors.

Throughout these past fifteen years, I still love the buy and hold strategy because it meets my objective of producing *monthly cash flow* and it builds wealth for our retirement in the back end because the equity paying down for the loan amount that we owe and maybe gain some appreciation when the economy is in the expansion phrase.

At the same time, I gain the most tax deduction benefits yearly. I now work 10-12 hours per week on the rental business, managing the property managers and helping them to screen new tenants because of my strong underwriting background from the mortgage business. I know how to access credit risks based on the tenants' income, credit history, and monthly debt payment, etc.

On a side note, we lost 80% value of our stock/bond account when the stock market crashed in 2000. After having all our assets once in the stock/bond market, it became easy to see that owning rentals that create passive monthly cash flow is a *much* better choice for us because we know the return on the investment is tremendously rewarding and predictable based on the economy data that we research in the area before invest. Rental properties are hard assets.

The stock/bond and most other areas of the market are fluctuating very dramatically all of the time. It can be quite scary for anyone who has a substantial amount of money invested there.

What This Book Can Do for You

This introduction is to serve as inspiration and a reminder to you that you don't have to stick with your boring day job that isn't helping you to make any money. When you are able to generate your own wealth and create a steady flow of passive income, *you* are in charge of your life.

I am proof that it can be done

My vision for this book is to help ordinary people like myself to build wealth buying one rental at a time using a safe buying strategy that I lay out in the book for you to follow from start to finish. I also want to save you a lot of money from paying for some real estate seminars that offer outdated information and most of the presenters are not active investors themselves.

I share with you all my wealth of knowledge that I have been using for the last fifteen years so you implement to buy your first rental and figure out whether it is right financial wealth creation for you and your family.

Some of you may even use it build it as a business while you're still having a full-time job so you can be financially independent sooner than working for corporate job. Think about it, you have to work five months just to pay for federal/state/social security taxes. You only bring home seven months of your yearly salary. How much do you have left after all your monthly expenses? Does your job allow you to live a life of your dreams?

How much sooner can you retire if you just buy one rental a year? By the tenth year, you will own ten rentals and each of them will produce $400/month. This will bring in $4000/month cash flow. With $48000/year, you can pay off the existing mortgage so that you can create more monthly cash flow, or use it for down payment of another cash flow property.

Can you quit your job with that monthly income? If not, what can you do to save more so that you can have money for a down payment for a new rental purchase?

I have helped some of my good friends buying rental properties. They have all different financial objectives.

Example 1

One of them had $200K set aside to send his son to four-year university and he did not know that he could use that money to invest in real estate and by the time his son finished four years, he would still have that $200K left. I shared with him my experience buying cash flow properties. He took my advice and bought the following properties.

He bought four properties, and each of them produced $500/monthly cash flow. So he was able to bring in $2,000 per month. His kid's school tuition was about $25000/year. This meant he only needed to add another $1000 out of his pocket for his son's tuition.

At the end of four-year College, he still has those rentals, which allow him to enjoy appreciation and tax deductions yearly.

Example 2

One of my friends was buying rentals because he and his wife had wanted her to be able to stay home with their young children. He had money in stocks and bonds, but that was not producing any income that would help him to reach his goal.

It was not doing anything to better his financial situation at the time. I helped him to find the path that would give them the financial freedom they needed.

Using his $300,000, he was able to buy six rentals. Each of those rentals brings in $350/month, with a cash flow total of $2100/month. His wife's income, while she was still at work, was $2000 a month. The rentals gave them even more than what she had been making

He was happy to find a solution for his wife so that she could be home with their little ones. When the children get older, if she decides that she wants to go back to work, they will still be getting all of that passive income each month.

Example 3

Another friend who worked a corporate job for fifteen years had a savings account of $400,000. He used his savings to put down for ten homes in 2007 which produce $4000/month cash flow income, and by 2011 he owned twenty properties that allowed him to quit his job, because his rental income created financial independence and also built wealth for his retirement by the equity paying down on the mortgage, and also the yearly appreciation that he gained. The best part was he bought his first ten rentals during the housing crisis, so the value of those properties were at 30% below market, and now all of them have appreciated 300% return for his initial capital investment. He refinanced cash out his first ten rentals and used those funds to purchase the last ten properties. He is now living the life of his dreams and focuses on some hobbies that he never had time to do while he worked at the corporate job.

This One's for You

I want *you* to be able to find these types of solutions for your own goals as well, and that's the whole point of this book.

Over the remainder of the book, we'll be covering the elements that you will need to know to get started as a rental property investor. It takes work and a good strategy, but I am sure you can do it!

It is easier than you might think to get started, so let's not waste any more time.

PART 1:

Rental Property/Stock Market

CHAPTER 1:
INVESTING IN RENTAL PROPERTY VS. STOCK AND BOND INVESTMENTS

While I was working at 3M, I did receive some employee stock benefits and over the two-year period, I gained about 9% return, so the return on my money was about 4.5% per year. It was quite a disappointing return, even though 3M is a stable company and the upper management of the company was great. I could not understand why its stocks were not performing at the higher rate. But I did not know what other investments I could make other than leaving my money in the stocks and bond accounts. I was just like a lot of you when we first start thinking about investing. We tend to focus on stocks and bonds and we never bother to diversify our portfolio beyond this. Herein lies the danger. Even though stocks have the potential for high returns and bonds can offer a level of income stability, they do have some serious disadvantages when compared with property investing.

Stocks and Bonds

To start, the price of stocks can rise and fall very quickly. This means that even though there is the potential to have a nice return, there is also a massive risk that you could lose a substantial amount of your investment – or even *all* of it – if you choose to use stocks as your only, or even primary, form of investment.

Even though bonds can be more stable than stocks and their prices will not fluctuate as much, the returns that you can get through bonds tend to be very limited. In addition, you generally need to hold on to them for a long time before you get to the point where you will see a return. In addition, if interest rates are on the rise, it means that the bond prices are going to drop. If you have long-term bonds, they will suffer the most from changes in interest rates.

In the following chapters, we will be looking in depths at the advantages and the disadvantages that these different investments can provide. In the next chapter, we will focus on the pros and cons of property investing.

It is important that you consider all of the pros and cons of each and that you try to build yourself a diversified portfolio that includes rental properties, as well as some other types of investments. Diversification is the key to staying afloat and increasing your chance of returns in the investment field.

Rental Property

Owning one or more rental properties can be one of the best forms of investment that you can make because it is relatively simple to make money, even when you factor in repairs and maintenance on the property.

Many Advantages

The goal of the rental property is to provide you with regular monthly income as long as you own it. When you have renters in your property, you will be charging them rent each month, and ideally, you will have placed the rent at a point where it is still affordable for the tenants, but high enough that you can pay your monthly mortgage on the property and still have money left over.

You should take a portion of your profit and put it into a bank account specifically for maintenance and repairs on the property. This will allow you to act quickly whenever the tenants have maintenance issues.

Having rental properties means that you will potentially have a highly leveraged asset that you can use to your advantage as well. This can make it easier to borrow from a lender in the event that you wanted to get another rental property.

Of course, you will also have a number of tax advantages when you own rental properties. Rental property owners can write off the interest on their mortgage, on credit cards they used to make purchases for the property, property taxes, and much more.

These are just some of the benefits of owning a rental property, and you can already see just how much it varies when you compare it with stocks and bonds.

Again, in the next chapter, we will be going into detail about the advantages and disadvantages of this type of investment, but this chapter should serve as a basic introduction of the main differences between stocks, bonds, and rental properties.

CHAPTER 2:
PROS AND CONS OF RENTAL PROPERTY INVESTING

As promised, we will be going a bit deeper into the good and the bad of rental property investing. For the most part, it offers benefits, but there will be some challenges along the way. As long as you understand those challenges and you are willing to face and overcome them, you will find that this can be a great way to create wealth and to provide some nice passive income.

Let's look at the positives first.

Tax Deductions

First, let's look at one of the things that is probably the most interesting to many of you. You will be able to deduct a number of expenses from the home that you buy and rent out, which can help to reduce the amount of taxes that you owe. Some of the expenses you are able to deduct include:

- Interest on the mortgage
- Property taxes
- Insurance
- Maintenance and upgrades
- Property management
- Utility bills if they are included in the price of the rent

Let's look at each of these a bit closer to get an understanding of what they actually mean.

Interest on the Mortgage

When you have a mortgage loan, it is going to accrue interest, and this can be costly. However, it is possible to make interest more bearable since you will be able to deduct your interest from the amount that you are paying on your taxes.

Property Taxes

In addition, you have to pay property taxes on the property that you own. Again, this sounds like an added expense that you might not want. Fortunately, it is also deductible, which can make your tax bill quite a bit easier to handle.

Insurance

When you own a property, you need to have homeowner's insurance. This provides an added level of protection to the home in the event that anything was to happen to it, such as a fire. The amount that you pay for your insurance is also an expense that you could potentially deduct on your taxes.

Maintenance and Upgrades

When you have a rental property, it's not as simple as renting it and forgetting it until it is time to collect the rent. You also need to think about the property maintenance as well as upgrades. The home may need occasional painting, new flooring, cleaning, landscaping, and all of the other expenses that you have with the home where you live. You'll also have turnover tenant expenses to make the rental property ready for new tenants.

All of these expenses are deductible.

Property Management

In some cases, you will take care of managing the property on you own. Other times, it is far easier to use a property management company, as they can take care of the bulk of the work and collect the rent for you. We will be going into managing a property on your own and with a property management company in detail later.

For now, you just need to know that if you do decide to hire a property manager, you will be able to deduct the expenses from your taxes.

Utility Bills

Some landlords might decide that they want to pay for all or part of the utilities for the homes they are renting out. If you do this, the money that you pay for the renters' utilities is deductible from your taxes as well. Something that you might want to do is run the numbers to see whether it is in your best interest to pay for the utilities and deduct them or to have the renters pay for their own utilities.

Another Benefit for Taxes

In addition, if the expenses are greater than the amount of money that you receive from your rental income, then you could deduct the losses from other income that you have. You could then reduce this total on your tax bill.

In the end, you can see just how many tax breaks you can get when you have a rental property. This makes it far more affordable to own a rental property than many people realize.

Of course, tax breaks are not the only benefits that you can receive when you have a rental property.

Depreciation

Depreciation is the value that your rental property loses over time. While this might seem as though it is a drawback at first, that's not necessarily the case. This ties in closely with the tax benefits. When you depreciate your property, you are able to deduct some of the cost each year on your taxes.

This doesn't mean that your property is not gaining value or that it will lose all of its value. After all, you can always make upgrades and improvements to the property. Remember, they are deductible as well. It's a winning situation all around when it comes to your taxes. Residential real estate property (1-4 units) can depreciate over 27.5 years.

For example:

The tax assessor's estimate of the land value is $45,000, and the building value estimate is $110,000. Your depreciation expense that you take each year against rental income would be $110,000 divided by the IRS allowed **27.5 years** of useful life (residential real estate) for a depreciation expense each year of $4,000.

You are able to deduct only a certain amount on your taxes for depreciation each year, though. Several things will determine how much depreciation you will be able to deduct. According to the IRS, these include:

- Your basis in the property.
- The recovery period for the property.
- The depreciation method used.

You are able to depreciate your property if it meets all of the following requirements of the IRS.

- You own the property.
- The property has a determinable useful life.
- The property is expected to last more than one year.
- You use the property in your business or income-producing activity – a rental property, in this instance.

Keep in mind that the IRS has rules about property that can't be depreciated.

Land

You are not able to depreciate land. The IRS says that "land generally does not wear out, become obsolete, or get used up, but if it does, the loss is accounted for upon disposition." In addition, you can't depreciate the cost of clearing or grading the land. You may be able to depreciate some land preparation costs, though.

Excepted Property

In addition, even if the property meets the requirements mentioned above, you are not able to depreciate it if it comes into service and goes out of service during the same year. In addition, the IRS rules state that you can't depreciate "equipment used to build capital improvements." You must add otherwise allowable depreciation on the equipment during the period of construction to the basis of your improvements.

Consider Getting Tax Help

As you can see, there are many different ways that you can benefit on your taxes when you own a rental property. Of course, unless you know a substantial amount about taxes and deductions, it can get confusing during tax time. You have to consider your rental property, as well as your own home and all of your other tax information.

Many times, you will find that it is easier and less frustrating if you simply hire a professional Certified Public Account (CPA) to help with your taxes. They will know all of the deductions that you can take, and they will make sure you don't make any costly mistakes on your taxes that would lose money or even worse, prompt a visit from the IRS. It is crucial to hire a CPA who specializes in residential real estate investments. They will know in and out of the tax benefits deductions. Their service cost can be higher than non-specialized real estate CPA, but having them to know all the benefits of rental property deductions, you will still come out ahead.

Equity

If you own a home where you are living in right now, chances are good that you have equity in the home. You might even use this equity to help finance the purchase of your rental property, possibly as a down payment. However, keep in mind that when you have a rental home, that property is also accruing equity as you pay off the mortgage.

This is a huge benefit for you, as it means your rental is working double time for you. Not only are you getting an increase in your monthly cash flow, which we will discuss later in this chapter, it also means that you will have equity that you could use to finance another rental property if you choose.

The interest rate on our primary residence loan is usually lower than it will be investment property. When you know how to structure the finance and let your primary equity money make more money for you on your rental property, then you are not just generating monthly cash flow from the rental, but you also have benefits with tax deduction, equity pay-down, and also appreciation when the rental property areas is in its expansion phase. You should consider doing thorough homework to confirm all the numbers of return.

You could also use the equity in one home to pay down another property that you own. You can do many things with equity in your property, including continuing to let it build.

When you generate more income from your properties, you can pay off your investments faster and build equity. The "equity pay down" will give you more equity in the homes, which you could then turn around and use to help you buy even more rental properties.

You can recall from previous chapter of how I was able to do cash-out refinances on seven properties because I had enough equity built up. Then I used the proceeds cash-out money to buy another ten wholesale properties from the builder.

Appreciation

While depreciation means that the value of the home drops, appreciation means that it goes up. A variety of different factors can affect the appreciation of a home, and one of the biggest is the location. In later chapters, we'll be talking in detail about how to find the best properties for rental homes.

For now, know that homes that are in neighborhoods near good schools, social activities, parks, and nearby shopping and entertainment are generally going to appreciate faster than homes that are in heavy commercial areas, or those that are in the middle of nowhere.

Another thing that you will want to do to help increase the appreciation of your home is to make sure it is always in good repair. In addition, you can make improvements that will add lasting value to the property.

This does not mean that you have to spend a fortune to do it, though. Think about the best potential upgrades for that particular property and the community where it is located.

You can look at the value of the other homes in the neighborhood and the types of upgrades that they have. Adding these will put them in line with the other homes, which can make it more valuable and that might even make it easier to rent out to prospective tenants. You can visit my website **http://korianne.com/resources/** to get resource links on how to search for comp able rentals of the area.

In some cases, you might be able to make the improvements on your own. Other times, it will make more sense to hire the professionals to come in and do the work for you. Again, we'll be covering this in more depth later in the book.

Leverage

As we mentioned, when you have a rental property and you are paying your mortgage each month, and perhaps paying a bit extra, you are gaining equity in the home. Your equity in a piece of property is what will give you the leverage you need to further your rental investment business.

You are able to use the equity in the home to help secure money for loans for other pieces of property that you want to buy and rent out. The beauty of this is that once you have those other homes and you are getting your monthly rent from the tenants that helps you pay down the mortgage, you are building equity in *each* of those homes. In time, this means you will have – you guessed it – even more leverage to get additional funding for more rental property purchases.

If you haven't read the introduction yet, go back and do so now so you can see how I was able to do just that after starting with a single property where we had built up $200,000 in equity. The next properties built up $370,000 equity in three years. The ten properties I bought 20% below market value from builder built up $440,000 in equity. These ten properties were valued at $220,000 each, but I got them for $176,000 each. I was able add 1 million in equity to our net worth after five years buying cash flow rental properties (the first eight properties equity built from appreciation and mortgage payment down and the last ten properties from builder was instant equity gained after purchased). I was able to build up the rental business value over 7 million while I was still running the mortgage company.

Let's revisit our earlier example.

Property Price: $200,000

Loan: $160,000

Total Down Payment: $40,000 (20% down) +$6,000(Closing cost)

Appreciation: 4% per year

That is a $8,000 gain ($200,000 * 4%)

Yearly cash flow: $4092
Appreciation: $8,000
Total yearly cash flow + appreciation = $12,092/$46,000 initial capital.
Return on investment (ROI) : 26.3%/ year

What Is Rule 72?

How long will it take to double your initial capital base on the % that you earn yearly?

72/26.3% = 2.73 years to double your money.

Can you earn this kind of return in the stock market for your money?

That is the reason why 97% self-made millionaires are real estate investors, because the leverage of the bank money and also the tax depreciation and tax deductions that stocks and bonds do not have.

Buying one rental home at a time can definitely build your wealth and can provide the time freedom that you desire for yourself and your family, as it has for me and my family.

I could not see myself staying in a corporate job or having another business where I have to trade time for money. I remember there was a ceiling of how much salary that I could achieve, even with raises each year, even though I worked so hard to prove my performance to my manager and also put in long hours.

The real estate business has blessed a lot of people to create financial independence and I am one of the blessed investors. I now have time to spend with my sons and also time to focus on things that truly matter to me and my beloved family. In addition, I have time and resources to give back to charities. My family loves to travel and I am so grateful that I get to spend 3-4 times vacation a year with our sons to show them the world and experiences for them to grow as extraordinary people. I have built processes and systems that the rental business can run on its own while I am traveling the world. I wanted this business to produce income passively, regardless of what happens to me and how I spend my time.

Visit my website **http://korianne.com/resources/**

or the more resources on how to analyze a purchase cash flow rental property.

Refinancing

Just as you can do with your own home, you can refinance the rental properties that you own depending on the type of mortgage that you have. However, it is important to remember that there are some very important differences between refinancing an investment property and the home that you occupy.

In fact, you should try to refinance a property only in order to buy another property, which will help you to build your wealth faster. This is the "cycle" that you want to follow – refinance when the property is appreciating so you can cash out and buy another rental. We will cover this more in Chapter 11 when we discuss financing your rental.

For now, when you are trying to refinance, you always want to try to get the lowest rate possible. However, when it comes to a rental property, you can expect to pay a higher interest rate than you would for your own home.

The reason for this is simple. The banks feel that if you were to get into financial distress, you would be more likely to pay the mortgage of your primary residence before you would pay for the rental property. Before you refinance, make sure that the rate you get is still low enough that you are going to make money on the property, and monthly cash flow is still there. You should try to select the longest-term loan possible so that you can collect more monthly cash flow and the mortgage payment is lower when the term of the loan is longer. Your focus is to create monthly cash flow and then build wealth in the back end when the equity paying down along with appreciation.

Take the time to shop around to different lenders to see what you might be able to get in terms of the rates. Get quotes from at least three lenders or mortgage brokers so you can choose the best option.

Monthly Cash Flow

The last of the advantages of rental property investments I want to discuss is the one that probably interests you just as much as the tax breaks, and that is the passive income that you are getting each month.

When you calculate the money that you will be getting each month, do not forget to account for the mortgage, insurance, maintenance, and other incidentals. The money that you have left over from that is the amount of money that the property is actually helping you to earn.

Imagine just how nice it would be to have this passive income coming to you each month. During your first year, you have one property. Let's say that it brings you in $400 a month after expenses. That's $4800 a year. The following year you buy another property, and it provides another $400 a month. That's now $9600 a year.

Even if you bought only one property a year for the next ten years, take a moment to think about just how much passive income it could provide! You could always do as I have done, and purchase more than one property a year. This helps you to build your wealth even faster. Make sure that you only purchase investment property produce monthly cash flow because it can sustain by itself regardless of the economy. Do not buy property with negative cash flow and depend on its appreciation. This is very risky strategy. When the real estate market crashed in 2008, there were a lot of investors were in trouble because they purchased rental properties hoping for appreciation instead of monthly cash flow rental income. The states that dropped the most were in Arizona, Nevada, and California. You can find out more about which states declined the most in 2008 at **http://korianne.com/resources/**

I had a few rental properties in those markets and I was hurt when the price dropped down to 35%. I had to sell them and cut my losses quickly.

What About the Cons?

As you know from the experiences that I detailed in the Introduction, I am a huge proponent of rental property investments, and they have worked out well for me. It's important to look at both sides of the coin, though.

Now that we've covered all of the advantages associated with rental properties, it is important to talk about the disadvantages. I want you to understand not only the pros we discussed, but also the cons. However, not all of the "cons" necessarily have to be disadvantages, as you can do things to minimize your risk and time investment.

When you know the pros and the cons, it will help you to make an informed decision of whether you should consider investing in real estate for rentals or not.

The cons that come to most people's minds typically fall into one of the following categories.

- Capital
- Time
- Preparing the Property
- Maintenance and Repairs
- Tenant Risk

Let's talk about each of these a little bit more so you can get an idea of what they involve and whether you are willing to deal with and overcome the potential problem. In most cases, you will find that the problems are relatively easy to deal with, but you do need to be prepared for some large problems along the way.

Of course, being prepared is the key to success in any business, and any facet of life for that matter.

Getting Your Startup Capital

Of course, one of the first things that will probably concern you when you are first investing in a rental property is the cost. How will you come up with the financing? You usually have to come up with a 20% down payment.

Fortunately, there are a number of things that you can do to come up with the money you need for your first investment, and it does not need to be difficult. After that first investment, you will be able to use equity and leverage to get money you need for future investments.

1. Yearly savings after your monthly expenses. Assuming that you can save $20,000-$25,000 a year, this will allow you to buy one rental at a purchase price at $100,000.
2. Cut down your expenses so that you can accumulate your savings account sooner for down payments. You can look into detail on your monthly expenses and see what expenses you can cut. You will be surprised at how much more savings you can do each month. When you have a plan in place, you can achieve financial independence in seven years or less even if you're still working at your full-time job. It is crucial to keep your day job on the first ten purchases; you will need to show your income to be approved for real estate investment loans. The lender wants to make sure that if there is no income from the rental property, then your job income can support for the monthly mortgage payment. Once you have achieved the monthly passive income to your desire, then you can with-draw from your job.

    I started this business while I had my mortgage company and it helped to accumulate our savings for the down pay-ments on the first few purchases.
3. A few of my associates refinanced to cash out their primary home that had a lump sum of equity which did not produce any income, which they paid at very low interest rate. They used the cash out money for the down payments and that was how they started their rental property investment from there. The interest rate payment for their primary home was lower than the return on the rental income generated, so it allowed

them to build their wealth sooner. The interest rate on the primary home is now at 3-4% and when you know how to buy a cash flow rental property with cash on cash return of 8-10%, you can make the difference of 5-6% on your money.

4. Seller finance option. There are some investors who started out with no money or good credit. They use this option to get them into the real estate investment, but this option will require a lot of their time and networking to find deals from motivated sellers who are willing to do seller finance option. This is another whole new topic for another book.

A Time Investment

When you get into this business, it doesn't mean that you don't have to work at all. You still need to put in the legwork when it comes to finding the right properties in which to invest. If you are going to be managing the properties on your own, this also means you need to be available to the tenants when they have issues that you need to deal with, such as emergency repair services.

Those who are taking care of the property on their own may not find handling the aspects of running the property to be too difficult or time-consuming when they have just one or two properties. As you start to get more rental investments, though, the time investment might become too much for you to handle on your own, and this would necessitate hiring a manager or management company for your properties.

It's very important to outsource some of the tasks to others so that you can have time to focus on buying good cash flow properties. The fee to pay for the property manager will take care of itself by buying good cash flow properties and also when you can acquire a property with a purchase price at 20% below market value. 90% of my rental business is running by property management companies and I spend majority of my time to acquire good cash flow properties at whole sale prices. All the fees are covered by the initial equity gain and monthly cash flow to pay for the property management service. I also spend 10-12 hours per week helping the property management companies to assess the risk of tenant qualifications when my properties have turnover tenants. You need to know your strengths and focus your energy in that area and outsource a lot of other tasks to specialized vendors to perform all the tasks that you do not enjoy doing. I knew a few good veteran investors who manage everything by themselves and they did complain about not having enough time to do other things. Being investor is different from being a landlord. My job is being an investor; I do not do the day-to-day operations of managing the property. I hire local property management companies to handle them for me.

Getting the Property Ready

Ideally, you will be buying properties that only need to have a minimal amount of work before they are ready to be rented. That might not always be the case, though, and it means that you might have to roll up your sleeves and do some DIY repairs. This takes time, effort, and some knowledge.

Of course, you also have the option of hiring professionals to get the place ready. It will still take time to get the place ready, but you will be free to take care of the other aspects of your business, such as finding the right tenants. Again, you could hire a property manager to take care of many of those aspects for you. This includes things such as collecting the rent and dealing with the day-to-day issues that your tenants might be having.

When you first start out, it is better to buy property with newer year built so you can avoid some high-maintenance costs.

Maintenance and Repairs

Keeping the property maintained is essential, and it does not come free. Whether it is landscaping, painting, replacing a fence blown down by a windstorm, or anything else, maintenance on the property will be your responsibility unless you have a management company handling it all for you.

If you don't maintain the property, you will find that your tenants are going to move out the first chance that they get. You want to have high-quality tenants who pay their rent on time and who stay on the property for a long time, as this provides you with some security.

The cost of repairs can get out of hand if you do not keep up with them. In addition, it is a good idea to set aside some money each month for emergency repairs on the property. You will not have to use the money from this fund very often, but knowing that you have it available can provide you with peace of mind.

If you use property management company to manage the property for you, then you can ask them to do annual property condition walk-though report. This will cost average $100-150 per report. This cost is very worthwhile so you can plan what big expenses are coming so you can plan for the reserve and not be surprised.

Tenant Risk

You might be very lucky and have only great tenants who pay their rent on time. Sometimes, they might be a little late, but if it is rare and they get back on track quickly, it won't be a problem. Most of your tenants won't complain about little things that don't matter, and you will hear from them only when there are real issues that you need to take care of for them.

These are good tenants.

However, I want to be honest with you. Not all of your tenants are going to be ideal. Some will pay their rent late chronically. Others may damage the property or disobey the rules set forth in the lease. There are any number of different types of problems that could arise, and you need to be willing and able to deal with them when they do.

In some cases, you will have to evict a tenant. You don't want it to reach this point, but it could happen. Before you get into this field, you need to know that you are willing to do this. As mentioned, property management companies can help you to deal with all of these different types of problems.

It becomes very important to make sure you are screening your tenants before you decide to rent to them.

Some of the things that you will want to look for when you are screening your tenants can include:

- Late Payments
- Financial Stability
- Lawsuits
- Criminal Convictions
- Evidence of Evictions

In Chapter 13, we will have a much larger and more in depth section on screening your tenants, the things you should look for, and following the law during your screening process.

Do not let the idea of dealing with bad tenants scare you away from investing in rental properties, though. Most of the time, you will not have any problems with them, and the benefits that you get are well worth the few bad tenants that you might eventually have to face.

You can find the link to use for tenant credit and background checks at **http://korianne.com/resources/**

A Mythological Disadvantage

One of the things that you might hear some people tell you is a disadvantage when you buy a piece of property as a rental investment is that you are putting too much of your assets into one investment.

While there could be some truth to this idea if you were to invest in only one property and never invest in another, that's not the way to grow your wealth in the first place!

The goal is to invest in *at least* one rental property each year. As you increase the number of properties that you own, this becomes easier as you have more income, more equity, and more leverage. When you invest, you can spread your rental properties into several different areas. This way, if one neighborhood goes south for some reason, you won't have six homes all in that area that start to lose value.

With diversified purchases of rental properties, you can mitigate your risk quite a bit. You can still have other investments that don't involve real estate, but I've found the most success for growing wealth to be from real estate, so that is where I put the bulk of my focus.

Consider some of the other types of investments that people make. If you were to invest a substantial amount of money in the stock market, as people do, it could be disastrous. A downshift in the market could cause you to lose everything, whereas with real estate, you have tangible property. You will find a good stable real estate market that will not be affected as much if the market falls.

What Do You Think?

Now you should have a good picture of the pros and cons associated with investing in property rentals. Overall, the pros greatly outweigh the potential cons, at least in my eyes. Ultimately, you will have to make the decision on whether you want to invest in this manner or not.

In the next chapter, we'll be talking about some of the other investments that people consider making – stocks and bonds – and we will look at the pros and cons involved with that.

I don't want to spoil the story, but I'm pretty confident you will find that rental property investments are still the top choice.

CHAPTER 3:
PROS AND CONS OF INVESTING IN STOCKS AND BONDS

While I believe wholeheartedly that the key to building wealth and securing your finances is through investing in rental properties, I understand that many people are still hesitant and that they cling to the idea of investing in stocks and bonds. It is something that's relatively simple to do, and many people invest and forget about it … until something goes wrong. That was the case for my family in 2000. We lost 80% of our account value because our investment advisor managed our account and he said he diversified it for us.

In this chapter, we will delve into the good and the bad aspects of investing in these areas. You don't have to give up all of your stocks and bonds – diversification with investments is good.

However, you may want to seriously consider what investing in rental properties can do for you when compared with these other investment options. I do also have investment account that I am now managing so I can share some thoughts below.

Benefits of Bonds

People like bonds, even though they aren't the most exciting type of investment you will make. In fact, some might even say they are some of the most boring! That doesn't mean that they are bad, though. They do have some advantages, which we will cover here.

- Safety
- Predictable Return
- Better Option than the Bank

They are Safe

You can't deny that bonds are safe, at least for the most part. With bonds, you are essentially investing in debt, which is safer than investing in equity (which is what you are doing when you are investing in stocks). When you invest in Treasury Bonds from the government, there is essentially no risk.

This means that you can put your money into bonds and never have to worry about losing that initial investment. It is not going to drop or disappear on you. That might sound comforting, and it really is for those investors who are most concerned with not losing their initial investment.

Please keep in mind that even though many bonds are considered safe, that *does not* mean that all bonds are safe. Some bonds, such as fixed rate bonds, can have issues. There are also junk bonds, and if you are investing, you would do well to stay away from them.

Predictable Returns

Just because bonds are safe does not mean they are lucrative, though. You might get an interest rate of only two or three percent. This isn't exactly going to win any awards when it comes to building your wealth, but it does ensure that you will get at least *something* as a return.

Because bonds are safe, they tend to be rather predictable. Many people who are getting ready for retirement like this predictability, as it lets them know what they need to do to prepare for their retirement.

Predictability can be good, but it's not going to make your bank account start to overflow.

Better Option than the Bank

Even though the returns on the bonds might be low, they are generally going to be able to provide you with a better return than what you would get in a savings account at the bank. Those who are saving money and who do not need it in the short term could benefit more by having their savings in bonds rather than collecting dust in a savings account.

Drawbacks of Bonds

Now, let's look at the drawbacks of bonds, some of which you have probably already guessed.

- Lower Risk/Lower Reward
- Junk Bonds
- Time-Consuming
- Cost

Lower Risk/Lower Reward

When you invest in something that has very little risk, you can't expect a massive reward. The world doesn't work that way, and neither do bonds. As we talked about earlier, the growth rate of a bond is very slow, particularly when you are choosing the safest bond options out there.

Here's the thing. They aren't meant to make you wealthy. They are meant to be a way to keep your investment money safer than stocks and to have at least some sort of return.

Junk Bonds

A junk bond is a corporate bond that has a low credit rating, which means it has a high risk of default. These are the riskiest bonds that you can choose, but if they pan out, they have the highest yields. You want to tread *very carefully* if you are thinking about investing in junk bonds.

Time-Consuming

Something else that you need to consider when you are investing in bonds is that it is not as simple as running down to the bond store and picking them up like you would some milk and eggs.

In order to choose quality bonds that are safe and that are right for you, it takes time and research. You might put as much research into getting the right bond as you do trying to find the right rental property to buy! However, you won't get all of the benefits that the rental property can offer.

If you are spending all of that time researching, don't you think you should get something more out of it than a measly 2%?

Cost

Many of the bonds that are out there are very expensive to buy. Even the government bonds that tend to be safer will often cost upwards of $1000 or more. Corporate bonds are even more expensive.

Now, you might be thinking that they aren't as expensive as buying a house to use as a rental property. While that might be true, you also won't be getting hundreds of dollars of passive income each month from having a single bond, whereas you will from a rental investment.

Pros of Investing in Stocks

Now, it's time to move on to stocks. To be honest, this is what most people think of when they consider investing. It seems simple and straightforward enough. You find a stock you like, buy some shares of the company, and hope everything goes well and the stock prices go up.

The key word in that last sentence was *hope*. Of course, before we get into the negatives associated with investing in the stock market, we should talk about some of the benefits.

- Appreciation

- Dividends

- Liquidity

- Diversification

- Choices

Appreciation

First, stocks have a substantial amount of potential. There is always a chance that the stocks you choose to buy can rise in value and you can see a massive return on your investment. The price of individual stocks will rise and fall, but over time, the stock market tends to go up.

When you choose to invest in stable companies, the value of your shares can rise. This is the main reason that people choose to invest in stocks. While all of this sounds wonderful, there is also the flip side to this that you have to be wary of, which we will discuss in the section on cons.

Dividends

Some of the stocks that are available will provide you with income. This income is provided as dividends, which are paid to you annually. One of the benefits of this is that the dividends will arrive even if the stock has lost value. The dividends are representative of income on top of profits that you would get if you were to sell the stock.

Many people use dividends as a way to shore up their retirement fund, or to help them with additional investments, which can help the investment portfolio grow.

Liquidity

Unless the stocks you choose have a very low trading volume, you will find that they are very liquid. What this means is that you can trade the stock or sell the stock very quickly. Investors like this aspect of stocks because it allows them to get out of a stock whenever they choose. For example, if they see the market starting to take a serious nosedive, many investors will scramble to sell their stocks.

Some even use this example as a reason to choose stocks over real estate. However, it's not really a very good argument in this case. You aren't buying real estate that you want to turn around and sell, so you don't have quite as much to worry about when it comes to the non-liquidity of real estate.

You are buying and *holding* the property, and your income is derived from the monthly rent that you get rather than trying to flip and sell a house for a profit.

Diversification

One of the other big benefits of stocks is simply that it is another place where you can make an investment and add to your portfolio. Diversification is always a good idea. Even though I believe that you may look into your investment focus on rental real estate, that doesn't mean that you shouldn't have at least a portion of your investment money in stocks and bonds. We'll talk about this more at the end of the chapter.

Choices

When you invest in stocks, you also have a number of choices available. There are over 2,000 publicly traded companies just on the New York Stock Exchange. You can find other options as well, such as mutual funds. Because you have such a wide range of choices, you can find a company that you like and believe in, and which performs in the way that you prefer.

For example, you might want to have a company that is stable and that seems reliable. You might want to choose to invest in stocks for a company that performs well when the market is on the rise.

Cons of Investing in Stocks

Stocks have plenty of cons as well, though, and it is important to look at those before you consider investing all of your money in the stock market.

- Volatility
- Time-Consuming
- Recovery Time
- Obsession

Volatility

This is the thing that everyone who invests in the stock market fears. It is the monster waiting around the corner, and it strikes often. Even when you have a stock that many would consider to be stable, there is no guarantee that you will not lose money. Just look at what happened several years ago with the stock market when everything went downhill.

Even though there's the hope – there's that word again – that your stocks will rise in price and that you will make a nice return, there is also a huge risk when you invest in the stock market.

If you have a substantial amount of money in a stock and the company starts to have issues, you could lose everything that you invested. This much of a risk is simply not worth it. This doesn't mean you need to avoid them entirely, but you need to have far more than just some stocks if you think you are going to grow your wealth and become financially independent. You should do your homework carefully and see how much can you live on with your dividend or annual return if you're out of job from your stocks account.

Time-Consuming

Just as with bonds – and any other investment for that matter – you need to put in the time and the research to know what you are buying. You can't simply follow the "hot tip" you heard at the water cooler and expect it to work out for you.

You have to make sure that you take the time to research the company, look at their history to get an idea of how the stock performs in different conditions, and you need to consider whether they offer dividends or not. As with bonds, you need to put in as much research as you would when you are looking for new rental properties.

When you put in that time and effort to find rental properties to buy, though, you have a far greater chance of making actual money each month, which you can save, or turn around and grow your wealth further. Even with all the research in the world, you simply do not have the guarantee when it comes to stocks.

Recovery Time

Let's say you decide that stocks are right for you and you decide to invest a large amount of money in a couple of those "surefire" companies out there. Maybe you do well for a while. Then, the market takes a dive and you lose thousands of dollars over the course of a couple of days. Maybe it is tens of thousands of dollars.

All you have to do is wait for the market to go back up, right? Correct, but it can take a long time – years, in some cases – for this to happen. Since you've lost all of that money, if you were to sell your shares right after the loss, you will never see it again. If you keep your shares and wait for the market to rise and the stock to recover, you could be waiting for ages.

Obsession

Here is another problem that many people don't talk about with stocks. It doesn't affect everyone, but there are a number of people out there who become obsessive over checking their stocks several times each day to see how they are doing.

This causes them to worry whenever there is a dip in the market and they lose money. So, they start checking the stocks more, trying to make the stocks rise by sheer power of their will alone – and we know this doesn't work.

Anyone who may have a tendency to become obsessive about something – anything – may want to think twice before putting a lot of money into the stock market. If you spend all of your time checking the market and worrying about your money, it's not healthy.

Why do people worry? Because they realize that the investment option they chose is entirely out of their hands. They can't control the market. It's generally a better idea to put the focus of your efforts into things that you can control, such as running a business where you rent homes and condominium units.

After all, everyone needs to have a place to live, and that means that as long as you have done your homework when it comes to choosing the right location and the right home, you can make money. Though my own experience, you have far more control than you do when you invest in the stock market. When you do your detail research before investing in rental property and its monthly cash flow it produces, then you're in control of your investment. You can do all your homework before making the purchase.

Should You Avoid Stocks and Bonds Entirely?

As you can see, there are good and bad things about stocks and bonds. In my opinion, you don't want to put the bulk of your money into those areas because bonds aren't going to grow your wealth, and stocks are too volatile to be trusted.

This doesn't mean they do not have their place, though. Having a well-rounded investment portfolio is always a good idea. Just don't rely on stocks and bonds for the bulk of your investments. Rental properties are the investment that can keep on giving.

PART 2:

Process to Buy a Rental Property

CHAPTER 4:
ANALYZE THE MARKET CYCLE AND THE SUPPLY AND DEMAND FOR RENTERS

By now, you've probably come to the same conclusion that I did. Rental properties are the best option for those who are seeking to create a *passive income* and who want to build their *wealth*.

Great!

Now, all you have to do is go out there and snatch up the first property that's in your price range, right? Hold your horses. We've already said that any investment worth making is going to require research, and that's certainly true when it comes to real estate. It's quite a bit more fun than researching bonds and stocks though, so don't worry.

In this chapter, we'll be covering all of the things that you need to consider when you are looking for a rental property to buy. Some of them might seem obvious, but others you might not have considered. All of them are important to different degrees, so you will want to include them all in your research.

There is quite a bit to consider, so let's get started. We will look at each of the following items on the list to give you a better idea of the things that you should actually be trying to find out about the areas you are interested in investing.

- Demographics
- Location
- Economic Cycle
- Job Growth
- Population Growth
- Local Industries
- Property Value and Condition
- Average Price of Location Where You Want to Invest
- Number of Listings and Vacancies in the Area
- Neighborhood Amenities
- Property Taxes
- Crime
- Construction Building Permits
- Natural Disasters

Get the Facts

Of course, I know this is a substantial amount of information that you have to consider when you are looking at properties. It can seem quite overwhelming when you look at this list, especially at first. This is one of the most critical parts of the process, though, and you can't skip it.

If you want to buy a good place in a good area that people will actually *want* to rent, then having all of the information so you can make a good and informed decision is essential.

Demographics

What are the demographics in the area? Some of the things that you will want to look for when you are compiling demographics information include the average age of the people who are living in the area currently, the gender makeup, as well as other information that we will detail later including economic factors.

The goal of the demographics is to give you a "big picture" that you will consider when it comes time to buy or pass on a rental property. For example, if you discover that there are fewer younger people in an area and that most of the older people who move into the area are buying rather than renting, it might not be a good place to put a rental property.

With demographics and other elements to help analyze the location and the market, it is like trying to look into the future based on the present. You want to find properties that have the biggest potential to be profitable. If the elements you are looking at in this chapter show you that the probability of the area being profitable for rental properties now and in the future, it could be a good idea to buy.

However, the future is not written in stone. When you do your research, though, you will find that there is a much higher likelihood of being successful. Now, let's get into the nitty-gritty details that you need to consider.

Location

You've probably heard this plenty of times before. Real estate is all about location, location, location. Well, the reason that saying is so popular is because it is true. Even though you might be able to find great deals on properties in nearly any city, that doesn't mean that it's always a good option to buy! Price is not the most important factor.

You need to think about things such as the city or town and factor in all of the other elements we will be talking about. You also need to think about the neighborhood where the property is located.

You have to go even deeper, though. What type of view is available from the lot? If you find a house in a good area, and even if it is a nice house, if it is located so that it has a view that faces something unsightly, then people are not going to be flocking to rent it. Renters are usually like the property close to all the convenient stores, easy access to freeways and close to good school areas. Buying in the middle price range in the area can help with renting it out faster because your property is in the average school district area.

For example: If the area that you're looking at the average price range in the same zip code is $200K, then you should find to buy property in the price range between $180K – $220K. It is in the average school districts and also when it is needed to sell, then you can sell it faster. I like to buy in the average school district areas because all of these properties are renting to family with children and they tend to stay at all this property average of 4 + years and they do pay their rent on time. Some of my properties are even renting out to tenants who have been there for over nine years from kindergarten to middle school ages. Even when it's time for turnover tenants, all of my properties can be rented in a couple of weeks. My vacancy rate is very low for all my rental properties because of the location.

Economic Cycle

As we talked about with stocks, the market can be impossible to predict. The same is true of the economic cycle. While it's true that there is a cyclical nature to the economy – it goes down and then it bounces back – you can't be guaranteed that it will follow a specific schedule. Sometimes, it will take years before you see a massive shift one way or the other.

This does not mean that you shouldn't pay attention to it, though. Think about where the economy is right now and what the experts say is likely to happen in the future – the course of the next couple of years.

While you can't predict what is going to happen, you can use past examples and current trends to get a better idea of how the market and the economy will behave on a national scale, as well as in the city or town where you want to buy rental properties.

If the trends and the predictions are looking positive, then you can invest in a rental with more confidence. However, if the area looks as though it is in trouble, it might be better to look at areas that are more stable, even if the price of the homes is a bit higher. It means that you will be able to charge more rent, so it shouldn't be too much of a concern, as long as the price is in line with other homes in the area.

In addition to the overall economy, look at the real estate cycle. A few years ago, we experienced a housing crash. While you should still be able to rent properties (people always need a place to live), it could mean that the overall price of rent that you charge needs to drop for a while as the economy and the real estate market right themselves.

You don't have to go negative with your investments, though. Simply dropping the prices slightly can make your property more attractive to potential renters.

Job Growth

You should also look at the area's jobs. What types of jobs are available within driving distance of the property you want to buy? Are there industries that are growing? If you find a property in a location that has a promising job market, this could be very good news. It means there will be more people moving to the area who need to find places to live, and they will often be looking for rentals.

Good job growth also means that people will be able to afford nicer rental homes, which is certainly good news for your bank account. Good job growth and a low rate of unemployment are essential.

Population Growth

This is similar to looking at the area's potential job growth, and they are tied together. If the area has been increasing in population, then it means there will be more people looking for places to rent.

At the opposite end of the spectrum, if there have been a substantial number of people who have been moving out of the community over the past few years, it could be an indication of trouble. Perhaps there aren't good jobs in the area, or there is something else wrong with the area that is pushing people away.

Ideally, you will be looking for a location that has shown positive growth over the course of the last two years. This shows that the area has promise and that plenty of other people actually want to live there.

Local Industries

Here is another area that is closely related to job growth. In addition to looking at the overall growth, you should look at the types of industries that are in the area, and those that are moving to the area. What type of employees will they need and how many? How stable is the industry? You should strive to find areas that have several industries that are growing, as this means more people. Strong industries also mean that the employees are generally paid well – although this may not always be the case.

While you can't predict what will happen with the industry in your area, you can look at other areas of the country. How have they progressed and changed the communities in those locations?

Some good and steady industries according to *Fortune* include:

- Oil and gas
- Airline
- Hospitals and healthcare
- Engineering services
- Management consulting
- Software development

Property Value and Condition

Of course, you also need to think about the property value of the investment you are considering. How much is it worth? While there is a price on the house or unit that has been put there by the owner and their realtor, that does not mean that it is the actual value of the home.

You need to find out what the actual property is worth, and you can find websites such as *Zilllow.com* and *Realtor.com* that can provide you with estimated property values based on the area and the other homes located there.

However, until you learn about the actual condition of the property, you will not really know what it is worth and whether you should make an investment. You should consider working with an inspector who can let you know everything that is wrong with the home, so you can get a better idea of what you should actually offer. We will talk about this more later.

Average Price of Location Where You Want to Invest

It is important to check out the average price of other homes in the area. Not all homes will do when you are trying to get a comparison, though. You need to look for comps, which are homes that are comparable to the one you are considering.

So, if you have a four-bedroom, three-bathroom property that you are eyeing, you want to look at the other homes in the area with the same number of rooms and similar square footage. Try to compare the amenities in each of the homes as well.

This will provide you with a better overall picture of what the average price will be. Check out several comparable homes – not just one or two – so you can calculate an actual average. This will let you know whether the property you are considering is worth the price, and it will give you a better idea of what you need to charge for rent to make money. It's crucial to average at least five properties within a one-mile radius of the property so you know the average price of the property you're buying. Do not buy property value more than 20% of the average price in the same area because when it's time to sell, it will take longer.

Number of Listings and Vacancies in the Area

This is an important one to consider as well. Take the time to look at the ads for rentals in the area where you are thinking about investing. How many people have places for rent? You should look first at the number of rental properties that are similar to yours, as this will be most important to you. However, you should also look at the number of apartments in the area. How many listings are there? This can give you a good idea of the number of vacancies.

If there are a large number of vacancies, what is it about the property that you are going to buy that is different enough to make it stand out? You need to make sure there is something about your property that will actually make other people want to rent it when there are other units or homes available that might be available for less.

Neighborhood Amenities

What does the neighborhood in the immediate walking area and within close driving distance have to offer? Is the house close to the beach or to some great places to shop and dine? Does it have some great local parks?

At this point, you want to put yourself in the mind of someone who is looking for a place to rent in the city. When you look at the neighborhood, what is it that entices you? Make a list of the amenities that are in the area now. Here are some of the things that you want to look for:

- Gyms
- Parks
- Movie theaters
- Public transportation
- Shopping
- Dining
- Entertainment venues (museums, zoos, amusement parks, etc.)
- Schools

This can be good in helping you determine whether the place is worth buying. In addition, you can use this information in your marketing materials when you are trying to find renters.

Property Taxes

While we already covered all of the tax benefits that you can get when you have a rental property, you also need to think about the property taxes. They can vary from area to area, and you need to understand how much they are, and how it will affect your taxes at the end of the year. This is something you will want to go over with a tax professional before you buy the property.

If the property taxes are high, that's not always a bad thing. As long as it is a good neighborhood and there is the potential for long-term tenants, it should not be too much of a concern. You can find the property tax information you need through the city or town assessment office or from your real estate agent who represents you in the purchase of the investment.

Crime

This ties in with location, but it's not always something that you can see easily just from learning about the neighborhood online--at least not unless you are specifically looking for it.

Nobody likes living in an area that has a lot of criminal activity, and no one wants to live close to a sex offender. Fortunately, you can find out quite a bit of information about the crime rate in the area through the web. Many local police websites will have crime statistics. You can also talk with people who live in the area about the rate of crime.

Look for trends. Has the crime rate been going up or down? What types of crimes are committed? How often are the police in the neighborhood?

Even though you aren't going to be living in the home, your tenants need to feel safe. If they move into a crime-ridden area, they aren't going to stay any longer than the end of the first lease. You can be sure that most prospective tenants will be looking up the crime rate before they sign a lease as well.

Simply choosing a safe neighborhood with a low crime rate can make a huge difference when it comes to renting out the property and actually keeping your tenants.

Construction Building Permits

Here is a good way to get a better understanding of how fast the area is going to grow. You can look at information from the area's municipal planning department to find out what new developments are coming to the area. For example, if you find that there are new business parks or malls coming to the area, it is a sign of growth.

However, you also want to look for developments that could conflict with your interests. For example, if there are several condo buildings scheduled to go up in the coming years, or if there is a project that will take away from some of the amenities in the area, it could be a bad area to invest.

Natural Disasters

You need to know what type of insurance you need to carry on your property, and understanding what types of natural disasters may occur in the area is essential. For example, if the neighborhood is in an area that floods, then you will need to have separate flood insurance. The same is true if you are in an area that should have earthquake insurance. Since you will be paying for these insurance costs, you have to factor in just how much they will eat into your profits.

How to Start Researching

So far I've told you the things that you need to look for, but I haven't given you any solid ideas of how to find the information you need. I've found that there are several websites with a plethora of information on just about any area in the country where you might be considering buying.

Check out my website resource page where you can access all the links to do your research.

http://korianne.com/resources/

Each of these sites offers a substantial amount of information on neighborhoods around the country. Visit those sites and take notes. When you are doing your research, you should be taking copious amounts of notes so that you can then weigh the pros and cons of the different areas where you might want to invest in a rental property.

Once you take the time to do the research for one property, you will find that the process starts to get easier. You will be able to develop a workflow that works for you, and that's great. It takes time, but after you've researched a couple, you will start to master the process.

The four areas that are the *most important to determine a stable market* are demographics, economic cycle, population growth, and local industries. Focus on these when you first start.

There is such a thing as doing too much research, though. You need to take the time to make sure you are buying a good property in an area that is growing and that will be strong when it comes to the rental market. However, you do not want to wait so long that you miss a good opportunity.

CHAPTER 5:
INVESTING IN CASH FLOW PROPERTY ONLY

This is very important chapter of this book.

Your goal should always be to find properties that are able to provide you with a good cash flow on a monthly basis. While appreciation is nice, and you certainly want your home to appreciate since it can allow you to refinance easier and to pull out cash to buy more properties, cash flow should be front and center in your mind.

When the property has good cash flow, it means that you are going to be making money each month. This helps you to pay down the mortgage on the home, build equity, and start building your wealth with passive income. Appreciation is important, but cash flow is king.

If you do not have positive cash flow, a rental property can become very expensive. If you have a negative cash flow property, meaning you are spending out of pocket each month for the home, the expenses will pile up very quickly. You will quit on this business in a couple of months.

Never invest in a property that has a negative cash flow, even if you think it will eventually turn around. The property needs to be capable of making money for you as soon as you buy it.

A lot of new investors do not actually take the time to stop and think about the unknowns in their investment. They do not think about the money they need to take care of unknown costs. If the rental doesn't have enough cash flow, they won't have any money available for those repairs and other costs.

When you are calculating the actual cash flow of a property you want to buy, make sure that it is able to account for any unexpected costs. Many landlords will keep a fund set up just for making those repairs and fixes as needed. Keep in mind that they are all going to be tax deductible.

Don't Depend Too Much on Appreciation

Appreciation is great. Having the value of the property rise means you made a good investment choice. However, you can't *depend* on appreciation for the rental properties. This is one of the biggest mistakes that many new investors make.

They invest with *high hopes* that a property will appreciate in value, but the property has little to no cash flow. This is more speculation than investing. Sure, the property might appreciate eventually, and it could be a good investment. Wouldn't it be better, though, to have a property that was able bring in cash each month and that could appreciate over time?

When it comes to appreciation, you should really take a conservative approach. When you are running your numbers, assume that the appreciation will be 3% per year. It might be higher than this, but you want to use a lower estimate, as this will help you prepare better. You can't depend on a massive gain, and appreciation isn't going to pay off the home any faster.

Cash flow, however, could, as we'll discuss later in the chapter. It all depends on what you do with the cash flow.

I lost over $500,000 when the market crashed in 2008 because I bought a few properties in the high price range areas--hoping the market would still continue to appreciate, the reason to buy these properties was to diversify my portfolio. I had to sell those properties quickly to cut my losses because they ate up my monthly cash flow. The rent income did cover the mortgage payment. It was a hard and costly lesson for me to learn. But I was determined to make that money back during 2008-2011, I bought 40 + cash flow properties at wholesale prices from small banks, wholesale investors, and bank-owned (REO) when I had a lot of choices. Most investors was scared to buy and some of them gave up the real estate investment career because they overleveraged and lost all of their assets. I bought these properties because the price was just perfect to produce the monthly cash flow of 15% cash on cash return on my initial investment that I was looking for. My patience has paid off in the last eight years; they all appreciated 40% of the purchase price.

Example:

Purchase price: $100,000
Total down payment: $20,000 (20% of purchase price) + $5,000 (closing costs)
Rent: $1200/mo
Total expense (interest,equity, tax, insurance, HOA, management fee, 5% vacancy rate): $900/mo
Monthly cash flow is $300
Cash on cash return: $3,600/25,000 = 14.4%
Rule of 72
72/14.4% = 5 years
It will take 5 years to double my invested money.

Here is the best part:

The appreciation BONUS:
40% appreciation from the last 8 years
Purchase price: $100,000
Now valued at: $140,000K
Equity gain: $40,000
ROI: Appreciation gain/total initial capital investment
ROI: $40,000/$25,000
Total percentage return: 160%/8 years (from 2008-present)

Annual rate of return: 20%

So total return on investment annually is 14.4% + 20% = 34.4
ROI = 34.4%
I was able to double our initial capital investment every two years and 1 month. 72/34.4% = 2 years 1 month

Can you make this kind of return from your stock/bond accounts?

Appreciation does come over time and I like to use **3% to be on the conservative side**. If you look at the historical of the yearly inflation rate, then you know US has an average of 3% inflation rate and it will cost more for builder to build new homes with the rising of the material building costs; therefore, your property will appreciate with the inflation rate. My ultimate objective of this book to show you how to buy your 1st cash flow rental property and then slowly grow your wealth from it by careful planning and smart buying strategy.

You can check out the historical of inflation rate from my resource page at

http://korianne.com/resources/

On another side note, I'd like to share with you a true story of my good friend who passed away when the real estate market crashed. He was a very successful investor with 10+ years' experience at the time that I knew him; then he became the builder at the time at he passed away. He built his development projects during the market crash in the area that have appreciated the most, but he lost his entire lifetime savings to the bank because his development did not sell to buyers. The entire real estate market of the city where he had his development was down 35%. There were no buyers for his development project because no buyer was able to pay him the price that he built. His hope at that time was to retire after his project was sold out because the appreciation in that market was crazy high—in the years between 2001-2005, the properties appreciated 10-15% per year. I sold a dozen properties at this city in 2006 at the peak price. I was very fortunate that I was running a mortgage business during these years to know the market was crazy, because the lenders loaned their money like an easy printing press to borrowers who had very little income. This was called a stated income loan, which meant they just stated their income based on the job fields that they were in. Some lenders even loaned to borrowers with no-doc loans, which meant that the borrower did not need to have a proof income--all lender needs is was for the borrower to have enough equity in their home to do a cash-out refinance, or refinance to exchange for a lower interest rate.

My gut knew something is not right and I shared my concerns about the mortgage business with him. I told him he should reconsider building, but he still hoped for high appreciation. Then in 2008, he lost his life savings to this project and killed himself. I was sad and speechless with the news. Since 2008, my real estate objective became very conservative. *I have a set of rules that I have to follow when I acquire new project, to meet my main objective, which is producing monthly cash flow. I have analyzed several thousand properties, but out of those properties, I only purchased over ninety properties in the last fifteen years. For every 20-25 analyzed property projects, I usually acquire just one property that meets my objectives. **You make sure the investment makes money when you purchase, not when you sell! It is easy to buy, but it is harder to sell!***

Appreciation is a BONUS!

What Is the Depreciation Deduction?

We touched on this earlier in the section on the benefits of buying rental properties for investments. Whenever you rent a property that you own to others, you have to report your income on your taxes. However, you can deduct rental expenses from the income to reduce the amount that you owe. There are a number of expenses that you can deduct, but depreciation works a bit differently.

Depreciation is when you deduct the cost of buying or making improvements to the rental property. The experts at TurboTax explain depreciation as spreading the "costs across the useful life of the property." Instead of taking one large tax deduction during the year that you buy the property, you would take part of the cost as a depreciation deduction, albeit smaller, each year.

Depreciating doesn't mean that the rental property is falling into disrepair, though. You are still able to depreciate property even when it is in good shape, and that's a benefit to you.

Visit my website to access the online tool to see the breakdown on the depreciation over the life of holding your property, with some basic data about the property that you're going to purchase.

http://korianne.com/resources/

Depreciating Improvements

Keep in mind that you will not only be depreciating the cost of buying the property. The money that you spend on improving the property is also depreciated. Some common examples of improvements that you could make, and which could be depreciated, include:

- Adding a garage
- Putting on an addition
- Roof replacement
- Changing the flooring
- Installing a new air conditioning system

These are just a handful of the potential improvements that you could make and depreciate. Regular maintenance and repairs, such as fixing a broken window or having plumbers snake the drain to remove a clog would be maintenance or repair, which are not things that you can depreciate.

One of the benefits of this is that you can take deductions to make the property better and more attractive for renters. This can entice renters, and it can convince renters to stay since it shows you take care of the property. In most of my properties that I purchased for long-term holding, I put in a few main upgrades like granite countertops in the kitchen and bathrooms. Over time, this cost will be covered because all my properties do not have turnover tenants often, and the bottom line is that tenant stability and depreciation compensate me for the cost of improvements.

How Long Does Depreciation Last?

You will start to take the depreciation deductions when you start to use the property to create rental income. The depreciation will continue until one of the following things happens.

- Deducted full cost basis
- The property is no longer in service

The full cost basis is the cost of acquiring the property. Therefore, if the cost of the property (including improvements and certain taxes and fees paid at the time of settlement) is $100,000, depreciation would continue until you reach that amount.

The term "in service" means that you are actively renting the property and making money from it. When it is no longer in service, whether you decide to stop renting it or you sell it, you will not be able to depreciate it.

Equity Pay-Down by Tenants Each Month

The money that your tenants are paying you each month is going to help you pay down the rental home and increase the equity you have in it. Having more equity in the house means that you will have an easier time getting a loan from the bank later when you are ready to buy a new rental property.

When you start to get more properties under your belt, you can use the profit from those rentals to pay down one of your homes. Many investors are able to pay off the homes in a fraction of the time that it would normally take. This means the majority of the money that comes from their tenants can be put into paying down other homes, or to provide an income for you.

Alternatively, you could decide to take the money that you make each month off of the properties and then save it until you can pay off an entire property at once. Some may suggest putting some of the money into the stock market, but we've already discussed how risky it can be to put too much of your money in stocks.

How Much Cash Flow Is Enough?

It is always a good idea to be conservative with your estimates on positive cash flow, just as you are with appreciation. Often, you will have better returns than you expected, but this is not always the case. By estimating conservatively, and by "saving for a rainy day," you can avoid potential problems, such as large repairs or having a vacant home while you are looking for more tenants.

By planning for the worst-case scenario, you can weather any storm without feeling much of a hit in the bank account at all.

The more cash flow the better, but it is important to come up with a good and realistic estimate based on the property, the area's demographics, and the average rent in the area. This can give you a better idea of how much you will be able to charge for rent. You can then deduct all of the other expenses that you have – mortgage, insurance, etc. – to get a picture of how much positive cash flow you will have at the end of the month.

If you find that you aren't getting enough based all of the numbers you run, then it might mean that it would be a better option to choose a different property that will provide you with more monthly cash flow income.

However, in addition to the cash flow, you have to think about the other benefits that the rental property will be offering, including tax benefits and equity pay-down.

CHAPTER 6:
INVESTING IN YOUR HOMETOWN – WHEN IS IT A GOOD IDEA AND WHAT DO YOU NEED TO DO?

You are probably already excited about the prospect of buying your first rental property, and you are probably wondering where you should buy. Should you choose a place that's close to you, or should you choose somewhere that's out of state--or all the way across the country, for that matter?

A Place Close to Home

I had my first rental where I used to live. To be honest, when you invest in your first rental property, it is a good idea to choose one that is in your hometown. There are a number of reasons for this, and one of the most compelling is the fact that it will allow you to see and understand the entire process of searching for, buying, and handling a rental property. You will be hands-on with the property, and I feel that is the best way to learn rather than simply investing and having other people take care of all of the details for you.

No Need for Property Management
When you choose a rental property that is in your area, you will also find that you do not have to worry about hiring a property

management company to handle everything for you. You *can* if you want, but when you have just one or even a handful of properties, you can take care of everything on your own.

This means you will be able to save on the property management fee, and you will be able to visit the property to see it as needed. Of course, it does come with some added responsibilities on your part, but that's all part of the job. You will gain a lot of knowledge when it's time for you to work with a property manager who will run the business for you. You will know the ins and outs of certain items need to be fixed, and also you'll have a rough idea of costs, so you're an informed investor. Some of the property management companies can be tricky because they even added their service fee on top of third-party vendor costs, so this will reduce your monthly cash flow. As soon as you grasp the concept of buying and holding cash flow property, your job is to work with people who know how minimize the expenses so that you can maximize your monthly passive income.

Run the Numbers

While I wholeheartedly advocate choosing a first rental property that is in your hometown, I understand that sometimes that is simply not viable. Just as with any property, you have to run the numbers. If the cost of a home in your area is too high, and if the demographics don't work in your favor, then it might be a better idea to look elsewhere for a home.

However, it is a good idea to exhaust your possibilities in and around your home area first, as it is going to be far more beneficial to you in the end.

The following is a good way to run the numbers so you can get a better idea of whether you should invest in a piece of property.

Let's look at an example.

Purchase price: $300,000
Down payment: $60,000 (20% down) +$9,000 closing costs
Rental income: $2500
Historical average appreciation: 5%
Interest rate: 4.75%
Management: 7% ($140)
Vacancy rate: 5% ($125)
Maintenance: 5% ($125)
Insurance: $1500/year
Property tax (about 1% cost to value of the house): $3000
Inflation (for insurance, taxes, expenses, etc.) : 3%
Property value growth (real estate appreciation): 5%
Your gross income (for tax calculation): $100,000

I round up the monthly expenses/maintenance fees to $390 (Including: management fee, 5% vacant rate and 5% maintenance).

I used the website below to generate the numbers return so you can plug in different scenarios from the link below

INCOME	Year 1	Year 2	Year 3	Year 4	Year 5
Rental Income	$30000	$31200	$32448	$33745	$35095
EXPENSES					
Insurance	$1500	$1545	$1591	$1639	$1688
Taxes	$3000	$3090	$3182	$3278	$3376
Monthly Expenses	$4680	$4820	$4965	$5113	$5267
Total Payments	$14640	$14640	$14640	$14640	$14640
Total Expenses	$23820	$24095	$24378	$24670	$24971
CASH FLOW					
Cash Flow	$6180	$7105	$8070	$9075	$10124
TAX DEDUCTION					
Interest Expense	$11115	$10948	$10781	$10670	$10559
Depreciation	$9818	$9818	$9818	$9818	$9818
Ins, Tax, Expenses	$9180	$9455	$9738	$10030	$10331
Rental Income	$30000	$31200	$32448	$33745	$35095
Total Tax Deduction	$113	$-979	$-2111	$-3227	$-4387
TAX SAVED	$35	$-303	$-654	$-1000	$-1359
NET WORTH					
After Tax Cashflow	$6215	$6802	$7416	$8075	$8765
Principal Paid	$3535	$3692	$3859	$3970	$4081
Property Value	$315000	$330750	$347287	$364651	$382884
Yearly Addition to Net Worth	$24740	$26244	$27812	$29409	$31079

Source: http://www.goodmortgage.com/Calculators/Investment Property.html

Year 1:

Cash on cash return: $6180/12 months = $515/mo
Monthly cash on cash return: $515/$66,000 ($60,000 down pay-
ment + $6,000 closing costs) = 7.8%
Yearly addition to net worth:
Year 1: ROI (Return on Investment): $24740/$66,000 = 37.5%
Year 2: ROI: $26,244/$66,000 = 39.8 %
Year 3: ROI: $27,812/$66,000 = 42%

Based on the ROI calculation above, you will get your initial investment back in less than three years.

You can plug different numbers into the calculator at the above link
and it will let you know what your monthly payments will be. You can
tweak the numbers so they fit your own situation.

The calculator will let you add plenty of other information such as
taxes, monthly fees (HOA fees or any expenses that you pay for the
tenant such as water and trash), loan term, inflation, and more.

The site will use the information to calculate a number of different
things, including:

- Monthly payment
- Cash flow
- Potential depreciation
- Holding period
- ROI (Return on Investment)

This is just the beginning of the information it offers. I suggest you
head to the above link and see how it all works. It will provide you
with a much better idea of whether you should actually invest in
the property or not. Don't invest in any property, whether it is in
your hometown or not, until you look at this calculator and run the
numbers.

Managing Your Own Property

As we mentioned, one of the benefits of investing in rental real estate in your own hometown is the fact that you will not have to go through a property management company. You can do everything on your own.

However, it is important that you understand what this actually means. Being a landlord can be a very rewarding job because you gain tremendous experience of running the whole real estate investment business, but it can be tough as well when issues/repairs arise.

It is important that you are emotionally ready to deal with tenants who may be difficult or who are late on their rent. In this chapter, we'll be looking at the types of things that you will need to do when you become a landlord.

In the beginning, it certainly seems like a lot, but believe me, *you can do this*. Plenty of other people out there have done it, and I know that you can handle it as well.

Let's look at some of the things you need to consider as a landlord. As always, we'll go into more detail on these after the list.

- It's a business
- Beware family and friends
- Getting the property ready
- Create a lease
- Preparing the reserves
- Finding the right tenants
- Landlord inventory
- Checking the property
- Marketing
- Dealing with problem tenants
- Know when outsourcing makes the most sense

It's a Business

This is one of the things that is hard for some people. In their mind, they know that they are running a business, but they sometimes let their kindness get the better of them, and this can lead to financial problems very quickly. It is understandable that someone might be late on rent one month. Life happens. However, when someone is chronically late, or when they are extremely late on the rent, you have to stop being so nice.

Their rent is what is paying the mortgage. When their rent doesn't show up, that means you have to move money from another location so you aren't late on the mortgage payment. You can't let this sort of thing slide.

If they can't pay, then they have to leave on their own or you might need to go through the eviction process. This sort of thing doesn't happen often, and you will find that most of your tenants are perfectly fine people who pay their rent and keep the house in shape.

You simply need to be prepared for those tenants that are causing issues, and you can't be emotional and take their side all the time. Remember; you are in a business now and your business needs to make money.

Later, we will talk about how you can deal with problem tenants and the steps you need to take.

Beware Family and Friends

You know how they say that you should never lend money to family or friends because it can cause problems down the line? Well, unfortunately, the same may be true when it comes to renting to them. Since they are acquainted with you and are your friends, they might get too comfortable being a few days late on the rent here and there. That's simply not acceptable.

You are doing this as a business. You wouldn't walk into their place of work and start taking from them, but that's exactly what it will feel like when they don't pay their rent on time, or when they don't adhere to the tenancy agreement.

You do not want to have this sort of tension with people that you love! Honestly, it is much better to have tenants that you do not know personally. This makes it much easier to run as a business.

Getting the Property Ready

Before you have tenants move into the property, it needs to be ready. This simply means that it needs to be clean, everything needs to work, and it needs to look appealing. You should complete this process before you start showing the property. Prospective tenants aren't likely to rent a property if the toilets don't flush properly or if the carpet is filthy, even if you promise to have everything ready by the time they move into the place. First impressions are everything, just like when buying a home.

Ideally, you will have bought a home that does not need a lot of work to prepare for the first tenants.

Keep in mind that when tenants move out, you will have to prepare the property again before the new tenants arrive.

Some of the things that you will want to look for when you are getting a property ready include:

- **Repairs** – Take care of them as soon as you learn about them so the problems do not accumulate.

- **Security** – You need to make sure the premises are safe and secure for the tenants. Simple things, such as security lighting, trimmed hedges, and the like can help to improve the security of the property, and they do not cost a fortune.

- **Landscaping** – Quality landscaping can improve the look and desirability of the home. Mow the lawn and make it look nice. You do not have to hire professionals as long as you have the basic tools needed to make the area look nice.

These are just a few of the things that you will want to consider. Every property is different, so think about the things that you will need to do to your rental property to ensure it is ready for the new tenants.

Create a Lease

You need to have policies in place in the lease that will determine what the tenants can and cannot do in the home. For example, you might want to have a nonsmoking home, or a home that does not allow pets. All of these things need to go into the tenancy agreement so the tenant understands their rights and their obligations when they are renting the property.

The lease also needs to include the type of rental agreement that it is going to be. Are you offering a month-to-month option, or do you require a six-month or yearlong lease? In addition, how much will you be asking for in the deposit?

Remember that the deposit is money you can't touch. It is protected while the tenant lives in the property. It is specifically for when they move out. If they have caused any damage to the property, you will deduct that amount from the deposit and give them back whatever is left.

Since most people want to get their deposit back, they will keep the property in shape and will try to leave it in good condition so it will be easy for you to turnover.

In the lease, you should also have a clause that describes what happens if the rent is late. You should always charge a late fee when the rent is late, as it will encourage people to pay their rent on time or even early.

You can check with your state law Federal Fair Housing Act if it is legally to charge tenants trip fee charge when there is a repair that is caused by them—this would not be for wear and tear repairs, as those are the investor's responsibility. Some property management companies that manage my properties charge a tenant service trip fee of $95/visit for repairs caused by tenants plus the repair cost. When tenants know there is a service trip fee, they tend to take care of the properties better. You should have this in the tenant lease contract.

Visit my website for company that I use to create the lease form:
http://korianne.com/resources/

Preparing the Reserves

Even when you have a property that you know will have a positive cash flow, there are still quite a few unknowns out there that you need to prepare for just in case. Perhaps there is a major repair that comes along and that needs to be fixed right away. Insurance might reimburse you in some cases, but it all depends on the nature of the repair. You have to have money in the bank that's set aside for these things.

In addition, you need to have money available in the event that you have a vacancy for several months. No one likes to think about this, but anything can happen. If you have the tenants on a month-to-month lease and they decide that they are going to move for whatever reason, it means you have to prepare for the home to be vacant when you are looking for new tenants.

If you are lucky, and if you have been conducting basic walkthroughs every couple of months, then you shouldn't have much to do to get the property ready. You might even be able to show the property while the other tenants are still there, which will reduce the amount of time between tenants.

However, if that's not the case, you need to have some savings for the rental property that you can rely on to pay the mortgage for several months. I like to have at least 5-6 months of mortgage reserve for each property. If the mortgage payment of one property is $900/mo, then I will save $5,400 for that property.

Finding the Right Tenants

This is one of the most important steps, and it is where many new landlords have issues. They don't spend the time and effort needed to find the best tenants for their rental property, and it soon comes back to haunt them.

The Main "Types" of Tenants

Not all tenants are good options for you for a number of reasons. Some tenants will make your time as a landlord a joy. They pay their rent, keep the property in good shape, and they are pleasant to be around. That's not the case with all tenants, though, as some are cut from very different cloth.

There are those tenants who end up having some real trouble in life. They might lose a job, lose a family member, or have some other emergency. It might make them late on rent once or twice. If this happens, and you are sure they are good people with good intentions, you can let it pass with nothing more than a warning. They will get things back on track.

And then there are tenants who you will come to believe were put on this earth with the sole purpose of making your life miserable. At least it will feel like this sometimes. Fortunately, these tenants are few and far between when you actually take the time to search for high-quality tenants.

How to Look for Tenants

First things first. You need to know about the Federal Fair Housing Act, and you need to abide by the rules it sets forth. You need to know and follow the rules so you are never accused of being discriminatory when you are screening tenants. You cannot discriminate based on:

- Race or color
- National origin
- Religion
- Sex
- Familial status (families that have children)
- Disability

Of course, you are a good person, and you wouldn't discriminate. It's still important to become familiar with the Federal Fair Housing Rule as well as the Fair Housing Rules in your state. This ensures that you don't do or say anything that could mistakenly be construed as discrimination.

Do a Credit Check

When you are choosing a tenant, you want someone who shows that they are financially responsible. While you can't take someone at face value that they are responsible and that they pay their bills, you can check their credit and check their income to make sure they are actually able to afford the rental.

The monthly income will ideally be three times what you are asking for the monthly rent. For example, if you are looking to get $1200 in rent for the property, you want the individual, family, or group to make at least $3600 a month. You can verify their income by asking for copies of their pay stubs, and you can also call their employer.

When you call the employer, you can confirm the length of employment, their monthly earnings, and even their attendance record. Why would you want to know their attendance record? It can show whether they are responsible or not, and whether they are actually going to be bringing in the money they claim.

In addition, you will want to run a credit check on them to see what their financial history looks like. Do they pay their bills on time? This will also allow you to check their income to debt ratio.

Check the Criminal Record

Criminal records are a matter of *public record*. This means that anyone in the public can view the criminal record at a local courthouse. When you look at the record, it will show minor offenses as well as serious offenses. To run the criminal background check, you will need to have the name and the date of birth of the tenant.

Something to keep in mind when it comes to checking criminal records is that some states will prohibit landlords from making decisions against renters for some types of convictions.

For example, you would be able to reject an application based on a history of violent crime or drugs – you don't want those types of people in your property. However, you would not be able to reject them because they had a bunch of parking tickets. Always check the laws in your state and abide by those.

Doing a criminal background check yourself can be difficult and time-consuming. You will find that it is generally much easier to hire someone to do a criminal background check for you and to provide you with the information you need. It isn't free, but many landlords feel that it is well worth it to have a professional take care of these checks for them. You will find that they can do more than just criminal background checks. They can also do financial background checks.

Visit my resource website page--there is a list of background check companies that you might want to consider when you are looking at prospective tenants. They can help to take the worry out of bringing in new tenants.

http://korianne.com/resources/

These are some of the best options when you are trying to screen tenants and to learn more about their financial and criminal history. Always check to see just what the screening company will cover, so you can be sure they are providing you with a thorough check.

Rental History

You should also consider the tenant's rental history when making your choice. It is important to speak with at least two of their most recent landlords if possible. The reason that you want to talk with at least two is because the current landlord might not be forthcoming and truthful about the tenant's history because they want to get the tenants out of their home!

Some of the questions that you should ask the previous landlords include:

- Did they pay their rent on time?
- Why is the tenant moving?
- Did they give a 30-day notice before moving?
- What was the condition of the property while they were living there?
- Did they cause damage to the property?
- How did the neighbors get along with them?
- Did they call to complain a lot?

You will be able to glean a lot of information from the previous landlords, and the answers to these questions can help you to make your decision. Even if someone makes a lot of money, you don't want to rent to them if they have trouble with their neighbors all the time and if they kept the property in poor condition.

Number of People

When looking for tenants, you want to make sure that there will be a max of two people per bedroom, which the Fair Housing Act deems as reasonable in most circumstances. The only time that there are exceptions to this rule are:

- State and local laws

- Size and configuration of the property

- Age and number of children

- Limitations of the sewer/septic system

You can determine the maximum number of people in the home, but not the maximum number of children. For example, if you have a three-bedroom house that also has a den that could be converted into a bedroom, you may determine that it would be suitable for eight people. This could be two adults and six children, one adult and seven children, or any other combination.

Something to keep in mind is that the more people there are in a home the louder it will be and the more wear and tear the unit will suffer as a result.

When you are choosing a tenant, take your time and think about all of these different factors. Putting in the time and effort now to find tenants that are the best for your unit is well worth it.

If you don't want to handle all of this on your own, there are companies out there that perform full screenings of tenants, not only background checks. This might be something that interests you if you don't have the time to do it. It does cost extra, but it can help you to find better-quality tenants.

Landlord Inventory

When you are writing your lease agreement, make sure that you include what items you are leaving to allow the tenants to use. All of these items are the "landlord inventory." In some cases, you might not leave anything there for the tenants to use other than the property itself.

However, you might have some items that are going to help them make better use of the property. For example, this could include things such as a washer and dryer, a refrigerator, a lawnmower, vacuum, and other similar items. Since you want to make sure that all of these items remain in the home and on the property when the tenant leaves, make sure you put it in the lease.

Sure, most tenants are going to be good people and they would not dream of taking these items that you left. However, you don't want to take the chance. Put it all in the lease, just to cover yourself.

Checking the Property

You own the property, and you want to make sure that the tenants are treating it right. You need to know if they are causing damage to the property or if there is anything that needs fixing that they haven't told you about. You also want to make sure that they are abiding by the tenancy agreement. For example, if you have a no pet clause in your contract, you can check the property to determine whether there are any pets living there.

When checking up on the property, remember that you can't simply show up unexpectedly. There aren't any "surprise inspections" in the world of landlords. When people are renting a property, they have a right to privacy. You still have a right to inspect the property, but you need to give them notice. Make sure you check the minimum notification requirements in your state and abide by them. You can set aside a couple hours' appointment with tenants to do at least one property condition inspection a year, to make sure everything is intact and the neighbors are happy with your tenants' stay at your property.

If your property is managed by a property manager, then you require the property manager to provide a property condition report once a year. They may charge you a $100/report, but it's well worth it to be aware of your property condition.

Marketing

When you are doing all of the work of a landlord, it means that you will need to market and show the property to prospective tenants. If you have never done any type of marketing before, this can be a real eye-opener.

However, marketing your rental property isn't rocket science and it doesn't have to be difficult. In this section, I will go over some ideas on how you can get your rental property out there and in front of potential renters, and how you can do it without spending a fortune.

- Advertise online
- Social media
- Traditional signs
- Advertise in print
- High-quality photos
- Video
- Referrals
- Start a blog
- Offer a bonus
- List with a realtor

Advertise Online

The internet has made things far easier for landlords who are trying to market their rental properties. There are countless sites out there that will allow you to post your property listings to make it easier for you to find potential tenants.

Some of the most popular of these sites include:

- Zillow
- Trulia
- Postlets
- Craigslist

You can also look for local property listing services on the web. Many of them are entirely free. Most landlords realize that they have these options available, and they happily post their listings on Trulia, Craigslist, and all of the others. Since it only takes a short time to put up a listing, add them to all of these sites.

Some, such as Zillow Rental Manager, will actually distribute your listing to the top rental websites, making it even easier to get the word out about your property for rent.

Do not make the mistake of *only* putting your rental property up on these sites and calling it a day. There are plenty of other things you can do to increase the visibility of your rental property and to make it appeal to tenants.

Social Media

Social media has changed the way the world communicates. It is easier than ever to connect with one another through sites such as Facebook and Twitter. Businesses have been making use of these sites to grow their brands and to promote their products.

You can do the same thing with your rental properties. You can post about the rental on your pages and ask your friends if they will do the same on theirs. In addition, you could actually take out highly targeted ads on Facebook to look for possible tenants.

While there are a number of different social media sites out there that you could potentially use, Facebook is generally the best option when it comes to marketing rentals because there is plenty of space for writing descriptions, adding photos and videos, comments and replies, and more.

However, you might still want to try out some of the other options that are available, such as Instagram. It makes it very easy to add photos of the property, and you could reach a different audience.

Traditional Signs

Even though the internet is important, you shouldn't dismiss the power of traditional signs either. Putting up signs in the window of the property that is for rent, as well as in the neighborhood, can get the property quite a bit of attention. The neighbors will tell people they know that a new place in the area is available and it can spread through word of mouth. Some neighbors might like to have their friends to move into the same neighborhood, so they will share your rental listing.

Advertise in Print

Another traditional form of advertising that you should consider is print. Putting notices in the local paper and want ad circulars in your hometown can help to spread the word about your property. There are still plenty of people who look through the paper to find rentals.

High-Quality Photos

They say a picture is worth a thousand words and that is certainly true when it comes to real estate. Good pictures will show off all of the features and amenities of the property. However, when you are taking photos, you have to realize they need to serve several purposes. They need to show the rooms of the property and the utilities and amenities, and they need to make the place actually look appealing.

While you could snap a few photos with your smartphone, it might be a better idea to put in a little more time and effort and *only* put up high-quality photos that have decent lighting.

The best option is to have a professional photographer take the photos for you. This is more expensive, but it is something that you might want to budget for. If you can't hire a professional photographer, it is possible to take the photos on your own as long as you have a good camera, good lighting, and are willing to take the time to make the photos look great.

When you have the photos, you can use them in all of the places where you market – the listing sites, social media, your own website, and more. Once you put them up on social media, they are easily shareable, which means your photos, and thus your property, can reach a large number of people in a short time.

Video

In addition to the photos, you might want to go a step above and do some video as well. Think of a video as a virtual walkthrough of the property. Consider what an advantage this can be.

Let's say that there are four prospective tenants interested in the property. In the past, this would mean you would have to schedule four different showings, only to find out later that the property just wasn't what two of the tenants were looking for. That's a lot of wasted time.

When you have a video walkthrough, all four of those tenants could watch the video. It will give them a good idea of what the property has to offer. Tenants will see whether the property is something that appeals to them or not. If not, they can move on. The two tenants that do want to learn more about the property can then schedule an appointment for a showing. You will cut down on the number of showings that don't go anywhere, and this can save you a substantial amount of time.

Of course, for this to work, you need to make a good-quality video. I'm not talking Oscar- caliber work, but you do need to make sure that the video looks good and is representative of what the property offers.

For example, you could do a walkthrough tour starting at the front of the house and then working your way through. Edit the shots together, play some royalty-free music in the background of the video, and then do a voiceover talking about the features and amenities, as well as some of the things in the local area that might be appealing to the tenants.

Make sure that you use a decent camera to take the video, a good microphone to record the voiceover, and have some calming music in the background. You can find royalty-free music online that is relatively cheap, and which you can use for multiple videos. The cost of getting a decent camera and a microphone is well worth it considering the fact that you can keep using them for all of your properties.

You could always hire someone else to do it for you, but this could end up costing almost as much as buying the equipment for yourself, and you would have to pay this fee whenever you needed a new video or needed an update for an old property.

Once your videos are complete, you can start a YouTube channel, and they can host the video. Then, you can share it on Facebook, your website, and more. You can also find other sites, such as the aforementioned rental sites, where you can add the video. The more places it is, the better the chance of prospective tenants seeing it.

Referrals

This is one of the tried and true ways of getting new tenants, but it is only going to work once you've been in business for a while and you have several properties. When you have a new rental home, or when one of your current homes is vacant, let your other residents know that there is a unit available. They can let friends, family, and coworkers know about it.

Offer a Bonus

Give people an incentive to choose your rental property over another one in the form of a bonus. It could be half off the first month's rent, for example. People like this because it will give them more money for the actual move and everyone likes the idea of saving money. As long as you have prepared, you can eat this cost for the first month. You really aren't going to be losing that much.

Let's use some simple numbers to see how this would work.

- **Mortgage**: $700

- **Rent**: $1200

- **Half of the Rent**: $600

- **Your Cost for the Promotion**: $100

When you consider the cost of some other marketing tactics, you can see that this really isn't much of an expense.

When you have promotions like this, it can attract some lower-quality tenants – not all of them, but some. Just make sure that you do your due diligence when you are looking for tenants, as we've already mentioned.

List With a Realtor

Another option to consider is listing with a realtor. They can help you to find renters, but this is similar to working with a property management company. You will be paying them for things that you could do on your own. Since you are in your hometown, you should try to handle as many of the tasks as possible. If you run in to trouble, though, there is always the option of working with a realtor or a property management company.

Find the Marketing Strategies That Work for You

The key is to make sure you are using not just one of these techniques when you are trying to market your properties, but several of them at the same time. The more "feelers" you have out there, the easier it will be to find potential tenants that want to rent your property.

As you get more practice, you will find the marketing techniques that work the best for you and for different locations. Use what works to see the best results – it is as simple as that!

Dealing With Problem Tenants

Sometimes, you will have great tenants. In fact, that's how it goes most of the time. However, there may come a time when you have problem tenants. When the home you are renting out is in your own hometown, it means you will be dealing personally with those troublesome tenants.

Of course, the goal is to minimize the number of bad tenants, and that is why I stressed the importance of screening your tenants before you offer them the rental property.

Remember to put down everything about your policies in the tenancy agreement as well. This includes late fees.

Here are some things that can help you when you have bad tenants.

- Be calm
- Be strict
- Be a record-keeper
- Be willing to evict

Be Calm

When you have a tenant that doesn't pay their rent on time, that causes problems with the neighbors, or that causes damage to the home, it is natural to be upset. You might want to yell and scream.

Don't do it.

This will only cause more problems for you down the line, and it will end up making the tenants angry and even aggressive in some cases. Your goal is to remain as calm as possible. When you are calm, you can think rationally and you will make the decisions of a professional. Shouting matches are *not* professional.

Keeping calm also helps you to maintain good relations with the tenant. Maybe they had a terrible month and that was why they were late on rent. Being strict, as we will discuss in the next section, is important, but so is being understanding. You just can't let it keep happening or they will walk all over you.

Be Strict

You went through the trouble of creating policies for your tenancy agreement for a reason. They are there to protect you in case you do get a bad tenant. You need to be willing to enforce those policies. The late fee, for example, is something that you should always enforce. If a tenant is late on rent, they need to know that they can't talk their way out of the late fee.

The same is true of all of the other policies. Violations need to be dealt with quickly. It shows that you are serious about those policies, and the tenants are unlikely to break them again.

Be a Record-Keeper

It is important that you keep records of all of your contact with clients, as this can help you later. Written records, through email or actual letters, need to have copies that you save. This includes the information that you send to the tenant and whatever they send to you.

Keep records of all formal and informal contact, such as maintenance issue requests, warnings, late fees, and the like. This way, you have a record in case the tenant were to say you didn't perform certain maintenance or didn't provide them with a proper warning.

Be Willing to Evict

Let's be honest. No one relishes this idea. Evictions can be messy, and can play on your emotions. This is especially true when you have a rental property in your hometown, since you might run into the people that you have to evict.

You don't want to put someone out of a home. However, you have to remember that you are only protecting yourself and your property when you do this. If it comes to the point where an eviction is needed, then there is a very good reason for it!

As mentioned, you can be nice and you can be sympathetic. However, you aren't running a charity. Whether the tenants are causing damage, not paying rent, or they are causing problems for the neighbors in the community and they are not responding to your warnings, the best thing you can do is evict them.

To do this, you will need to have the help of a qualified attorney who understands the process and who can help you each step of the way. Make sure the attorney is in your hometown, or at least nearby, as you will likely need to meet with them.

I suggest that you start to look for an attorney even before you rent the property the first time, just so you know whom to call in the event that things turn sour in a few months. Many will provide you with a free consultation so you can learn more about the process. If the need for an eviction does arise, you will be able to call them and you will already know what comes next.

Know When Outsourcing Makes the Most Sense

Sometimes, you might not have any luck when it comes to renting the property. You might have trouble with the marketing, or you might not be able to give the rental property as much attention as it actually deserves.

If you find yourself in this situation, you may want to consider out-sourcing for some of the tasks that you can't handle on your own. It will cost you and eat away at some of your profits, so I feel the best option is to get to a point where you are comfortable and confident in taking care of the different jobs that need to be done.

This doesn't mean that you need to become a plumber, an electrician, and the like. When there are repairs, you will contact professionals who can come in and take care of the repairs and maintenance. However, it does mean that you can improve your marketing skills, your photography skills, your video editing, and other elements that can help with the process.

Taking Care of Business

When you have your first rental in your hometown, it is going to be a valuable learning experience. As you've seen in this chapter, there's a lot to learn about and a lot that you will have to do. It can be fun, though, and you don't *need* to hire a property manager.

However, you might eventually want to expand your reach beyond your hometown, and that's the focus of the next chapter.

CHAPTER 7:

INVESTING IN REAL ESTATE RENTALS OUTSIDE OF YOUR TOWN AND EVEN OUTSIDE OF YOUR STATE

Let's say you have a couple of rental properties in your hometown and things are going well. You are making money, building equity, and paying down those homes. However, you want to do more. You want to expand, but you don't want to keep buying in your town, or even in the next town over.

You want to see what's farther out in the state. You want to check out some properties that are in other states.

The main reason is return on investment (ROI) is higher than your state.

Will this work?

What are you supposed to do differently?

As always, it is all about the financials. Does it make sense financially to buy property that you won't be able to visit often and that you aren't going to be able to manage as easily on your own?

First, let's get a better understanding of the price to rent ratio.

The Price to Rent Ratio (Yield)

The price to rent ratio is a type of mathematical calculation that factors in the total costs of homeownership against the cost of renting a property. The total costs of ownership that need to be included when calculating the ratio are:

- Mortgage and principal interest
- Property taxes
- Insurance
- Closing costs
- HOA dues (if applicable)
- Mortgage insurance (if needed)

You can divide the median home prices and the median rents for a particular area to come up with the ratio. According to Investopedia, "At the peak of the US market in 2006, the ratio for the US was 18.46. The ratio dropped to 11.34 by the end of 2010. The Long-term average, from '89 to '03 was 9.56." Generally, it is best to buy when the ratio is under 15.

Markets that have a high price to rent ratio are not usually good options for an investment.

An Example of a Good Financial Investment

Here's an example that will show you the *types* of numbers that you will want to look for when you are choosing a property.

Property Price: $150,000

Rental Income: $1500/month

Rent Value to Price Ratio: 1%

My minimum requirement when I consider buying a property is that it must have a rental yield of at least 1% of total cost of the property.

Rental yield greater than 1% is even better, but most of these areas are very stable markets and you will see less appreciation increase over time.

You need to make sure that the property will produce a good monthly cash flow, remembering that in these cases you might need to hire a property management company to take care of the tasks of screening tenants, marketing, renting, collecting rent, and more. You need to have enough cash flow to cover the expense of a property management company and still have positive cash flow.

You will find that there are actually a number of benefits when it comes to investing in property that's not in your hometown.

- Tackle a developing market
- Better taxes
- More options
- Levels of demand

Your main objective when purchasing a rental property is making sure the monthly cash flow meets your requirement and the rental market is strong, with the percentage of renters in the city that you're going to invest in at 40% or higher. I know my property will not be vacant long between tenant turnovers.

Visit my website resource page to get access to percent of housing unit occupied by renters by major city where you're going to invest.

Tackle a Developing Market

The real estate market can vary greatly in different areas of your state and all across the country, for that matter. If you are keeping up with real estate news – as you should be – then you can learn about some areas that are growing quickly and that could be good areas for investment.

Of course, you will also have to conduct all of the same type of research as when you are buying in your hometown. It needs to make financial sense, and it needs to be a good property.

Some of the things that you should look for when you are trying to find developing areas include:

- Business development in different areas
- Infrastructure improvements

Investing in these areas early can be a great idea for several reasons. It means that more people will be moving to the area as it becomes more desirable. Property values tend to rise as well, so you may have more appreciation in the home.

Better Taxes

You might also find that there are even more tax advantages in other states. States all have different tax regulations, and you might find that some are able to save you more money each year than others.

Check out the tax regulations in the different states that have properties that interest you. The taxes aren't necessarily a make or break point, but they are definitely something that you will want to consider. As always, it's about the numbers at the end of the day.

More Options

Of course, when you are investing in other locations, it means you have more options and more opportunities. In some areas, the price of homes will be lower, which could mean that you can afford better properties, or more properties than in your own hometown. Keep in mind that if the properties cost less, it could mean that the cost of rentals is lower on average as well.

As long as you are still able to pull in a good percentage of positive cash flow though, it can be a good investment option for you.

Levels of Demand

Different locations have different levels of demand for rentals. Towns with large industries, as well as college towns, tend to have a higher level of demand for rental properties. This means it is often easier to find tenants in these locations.

If you are thinking of investing in a college town, though, you need to be aware that the housing tends to be seasonal and it slows down in between semesters. This could mean that you have to find renters more frequently, or that you will have a vacant home for part of the year, neither of which is ideal.

Some of the other locations that have higher levels of demand are those cities that have tech parks and business parks, for example. These tend to be better than college towns simply because the tenants seem to stay in one place for longer. They aren't necessarily sure they want to buy a home in the area, but they need to be there for their job.

The Challenges to Consider

When you are investing in an out-of-state market, there will certainly be some challenges that you need to face. Understanding these challenges can help you determine whether you are ready to move beyond the bounds of your state or if you would be better served continuing to buy property closer to your hometown.

- More research needed
- Different laws
- Contacts needed

More Research Needed

When you are investing in an out-of-state property, you don't have the same familiarity that you do when buying in your own backyard. You don't know what the economic conditions are in certain towns, and a "great" price on a home might turn out to be a property that is impossible to rent. You don't know the good neighborhoods from the bad ones.

This just means is that you need to do more research. In fact, you will need to do a lot more research. You should look at any community web-sites and blogs, Facebook pages, statistics, and other information that you can to get a better insight into what the area offers and what it lacks.

There is no such thing as too much research in this case.

Different Laws

Trying to understand all of the laws and regulations that are in place in other states can be difficult as well. Even when you read the laws and regulations, your research might not always match up to how things actually happen in those areas.

Your best bet is to try to talk with other homeowners in the area, as well as real estate professionals, to get a better idea of what it's like. For example, if you buy a property and then want to put on a small addition of another bedroom to make it easier to rent, what type of red tape do you have to cut through to do it?

Again, research will help in this matter, and make sure you ask plenty of questions when you start to talk with real estate agents. Most of the time, you will find that the regulations are straightforward and won't really hamper you, but it is better to be safe now rather than sorry later.

Contacts Needed

Once you have a couple of properties set up in your own home-town, you probably have all of the contacts you need. You have a landscaping crew that can come out and take care of the lawn. You have plumbers and electricians that you know and trust. You have an attorney that you can call just in case you need some legal advice or need to start the eviction process. You have a network of people that you can call when you need them.

When you are in another state, you don't have any of those things set up. It means that you have to build a network there as well. You can do it, but it will just take some more time and effort on your part.

What's the Decision Going to Be?

Ultimately, the decision of whether you should invest in out-of-state property will be based on your comfort levels. How do you feel about not being able to reach your property easily and not being able to take care of everything on your own?

We will be talking more about hiring a property manager in a later chapter. When you have a distant rental property, this makes a lot of sense. You just need to make sure that you are choosing a reputable property management company, as there are some bad ones out there.

Look at the numbers. You are probably sick of hearing that by now, but that's what it all comes down to in the end. You need to make sure that you will be able to make a profit on the property that you buy. If the numbers pan out, and if you are willing to let property managers handle the bulk of the work for a fee, then you should consider investing outside of your state.

I personally like to invest in states that produce me the highest on the monthly cash flow with strong job growth area. I found out the ROI is higher after subtracting the local property manager fee. In most of the states where housing prices are high, the rental income is low. Therefore, cash on cash return on my initial capital investment returns is about 3-4%. Examples include California, Washington State, New York, and Washington.

Let look at an example below at higher purchase price with lower rental income.
Purchase price: $400,000
Down payment: $90,000 (20% down) +$10,000 closing cost
Rental income: $3000
Historical average appreciation: 5%
Interest rate: 4.75%
Monthly expenses/maintenance fees (management, vacancy, and maintenance): $600
Insurance: $1500/year
Property tax (about 1% cost to value of the house) : $4000
Inflation (for insurance, taxes, expenses, ect) : 3%

Property value growth (real estate appreciation): 5%
Your gross income (for tax calculation): $100,000.00

INCOME	Year 1	Year 2	Year 3	Year 4	Year 5
Rental Income	$36000	$37440	$38937	$40495	$42114
EXPENSES					
Insurance	$1500	$1545	$1591	$1639	$1688
Taxes	$4000	$4120	$4243	$4370	$4502
Monthly Expenses	$7200	$7416	$7638	$7867	$8103
Total Payments	$19404	$19404	$19404	$19404	$19404
Total Expenses	$32104	$32485	$32876	$33280	$33697
CASH FLOW					
Cash Flow	$3896	$4955	$6061	$7215	$8417
TAX DEDUCTION					
Interest Expense	$14725	$14504	$14283	$14136	$13988
Depreciation	$13090	$13090	$13090	$13090	$13090
Ins, Tax, expenses	$12700	$13081	$13472	$13876	$14293
Rental Income	$36000	$37440	$38937	$40495	$42114
Total Tax Deduction	$4515	$3235	$1908	$607	$-743
TAX SAVED	$1399	$1002	$591	$188	$-230
NET WORTH					
After Tax Cash flow	$5295	$5957	$6652	$7403	$8187
Principal Paid	$4679	$4900	$5121	$5268	$5416
Property Value	$420000	$441000	$463050	$486202	$510512
Yearly Addition to Net Worth	$29974	$31857	$33823	$35823	$37913

Source: http://www.goodmortgage.com/Calculators/Investment_Property.html

Cash on cash return: $3896/12months = $324.67/mo
Total investment: $90,000 ($80,000 down payment + $10,000 closing cost)
Monthly cash on cash return: $324.67/$90,000 = 3.6%.

You can revisit page 68 to compare the purchase price and the rental income difference. The cash on cash return is at 8.4% on the lower price purchase property.

CHAPTER 8:
TYPES OF RESIDENTIAL PROPERTIES

This chapter is going to be short and sweet. We will be looking at the different types of residential properties in which you can invest. Some, as you will soon see, are better than others.

- Single family
- Townhouse
- Condo
- Duplex
- Triplex
- Fourplex

Single Family

The definition of a single-family home is simple. It is a home that's individual and freestanding, and which is not attached to another dwelling. It is generally on a lot that's larger than the size of the home. Lot sizes can differ greatly, though.

This is my favorite type of investment property for a number of reasons. First, single- family homes appreciate the most, which means you can get more bang for your buck, so to speak. In addition, these properties tend to attract better-quality tenants since they are typically more expensive to rent. You will often find young families who will want to rent these types of homes, and the average stay in the homes is five years.

You just need to make sure that you choose a single-family home that's located in a good neighborhood with a decent school district. Ideally, you will want to find a four-bedroom, two-bathroom home in middle-income areas.

These types of properties are very appealing, and I've found that they are easy to rent and to find great tenants.

Of course, that's not the only option you have. It's just the one that I consider the best and the easiest for you to maintain.

Townhouse

A townhouse is a home that is attached side by side to other homes in a row. They tend to be at least two stories high, and they are narrow. They are also uniform with the other townhomes that are connected to them. When you are buying these, you will generally buy only one townhouse, while the other homes to either side are owned by different people.

This is not necessarily a bad option, but there are some negatives to it. Most of these types of properties are part of a homeowner's association. This means that you will have to pay the monthly HOA dues. This can eat into your profits. You could add the cost onto the rent, but that could raise the price of rent so high that no one wants to rent the place!

These types of units will appreciate less than a single-family home in most cases. It is generally young couples that rent these types of properties, and they stay for an average of two to three years.

Condominium

Condominiums have quite a few similarities to both townhouses and apartment buildings. They are units that are side-by-side, and often stacked on top of one another. Since much of the structure includes shared areas, such as the wall, roof, and common areas, it could mean a little less in maintenance costs, since they are shared among homeowners.

However, you also have a homeowners' association (HOA) with condominiums, and that means less profit for you. It also means that they may have more restrictions on the things that tenants can and can't do. For example, you might be okay with your tenants having a cat, but pets might be against the HOA policy. They also want uniformity between the units, so you can't do anything that helps your property stand out.

They also appreciate less than a single-family home, and you will find that most of the people renting these are also younger couples or roommates who move within a couple of years.

Duplex, Triplex, Fourplex

I've decided to talk about all of these in the same section because they are so similar. The only real difference is the number of units that you will own in a building. A duplex will have two units in a building. A triplex will have three, and a will have four. When you buy these properties, you are buying the entire building.

At first blush, this might seem like a great idea. You can buy a single property and then have two to four families living there. It seems like that would mean that you get quite a bit more in rent. You have to keep a few things in mind, though, as these are not your best option – not by a long shot.

For starters, the cost of the building will generally be higher since you are buying all of the units, so you will not see as much in profits as you think. The buildings only appreciate at the cap rate as well. You will be spending more and the buildings will only gain a limited amount of value.

In addition, the monthly maintenance costs on these properties is much higher than it is with the other options. It can seem as though you always have people coming to fix one problem or another.

You also need to consider the fact that you will have several families living in close proximity to one another. What do you do if they don't get along or cause problems with one another? It can be a nightmare trying to defuse arguments and play peacemaker without taking sides.

These buildings are generally in areas of town that are less desirable and that some people will consider rough. Because of this, there cost of the average rent in the area is lower, and this means even less profit for you.

The tenants tend to move frequently, which means you will spend a lot of time trying to find new people to rent the property. In addition, tenants do not usually keep up with the property, so you will likely have more costs associated with maintenance and cleaning.

You could end up spending a large amount of time managing these properties due to all of these factors, and suddenly that passive income you've been trying to earn doesn't seem quite so passive anymore.

If you are new to investing, it is in your best interest to put this option at the bottom of your list of possibilities. The headaches that can come with it simply aren't worth the meager money that you can make.

What's Right for You?

I've already told you which of these is my favorite – the single-family home. I suggest that this is where you start when you are getting into this business. One of the only issues with this is that the cost is typically going to be higher than if you were to choose a condo or a townhome.

If you don't have the money to invest in a single-family home currently, and you are eager to get started, you could choose one of the other options on the list. Just make sure that you run the numbers properly and factor in things such as HOA fees so you can be sure you are going to make a nice profit at the end of the day.

Holding off for a bit until you can afford a single-family home as your investment is generally a good idea, I feel. You will be much happier with the results. Once you start to make money with several properties, you might want to branch out into other types of residential properties, such as condos or a townhouse.

I still suggest staying away from the duplexes, triplexes, and four-plexes out there, at least for now. Get quite a bit of experience under your belt and make sure it is going to be capable of making a profit for you without taking up all of your time.

I like single-family home for all the reasons I've already outlined, plus this one: when it's time to sell, you can sell it faster. New buyers will look into buying a single-family home first because they would like to avoid the homeowners' association costs, and if they do their homework, they'll also know that the appreciation rate is greatest for a single-family home. Most renters with children prefer to rent a place with yard for their children and they will stay at your home longer until their children are out of those school districts. I have owned numerous homes, and tenants stayed over 7 + years on a lease. How nice to pay off the property when you need to deal with only four to five tenant turnovers when you follow the screening guidelines to approve a tenant.

CHAPTER 9:
PURCHASE STRATEGIES

Now, we are getting to the point where you will need to start thinking about *how* you will be making your purchases and what strategies you might want to consider. There are essentially five different options, and we will be covering each of them in this chapter.

- Retail purchase
- Wholesale property
- Buying bulk from your local bank
- Owner financing
- Bank-owned property (REO)

Retail Purchase

This is what people generally think of when it comes to buying property. They buy the property at market value. This is definitely a workable option, but it has to make sense from a financial perspective. Remember, you aren't buying your dream home, you are buying a property that needs to make money.

Whenever I buy a house at the market value, I need to know that the cost to income ratio is equal to or greater than 1%. Check out the following example to see how this needs to work.

Home value: $300k

Purchase price: $300k

Rental income: $3000/month

Rent value to price ratio: = $3,000/$300,000 = 1%

When the income generates 1% of the purchase price, you know you have good monthly cash flow. The cash on cash return will average between 8-10%.

Wholesale Properties

Buying wholesale properties can actually be a BEST option. They are rarer than many other types of properties, but there are some out there, and I encourage you to look for them. Here are the basics of how they work.

First, keep in mind that these wholesale homes are generally the types of homes that people get and flip. However, you won't be flipping it. You will be getting it ready as a rental property. These types of properties will generally require a full cash purchase, or you will need to have enough equity down so you can get a hard money loan to buy it outright.

Wholesale properties are offered though wholesale investors; bank-owned property (REO), bulk REO properties are offered through small banks or as short sale properties.

80% of my purchase transactions have been bought at wholesale prices since 2005. This strategy does involve extensive technical process and more third parties:

Wholesale investors who only want to earn **finder fees**; they're the middle person to connect desperate sellers and buy/hold investors or property flippers. *Purchasing wholesale properties is the faster way to build your wealth. You don't get just higher monthly cash flow because your rent to price ratio is greater than 1%. You also add instant equity to your net worth right after closing without waiting for the property to appreciate over time.*

You can make your first 50-75% percent return for your down payment as soon as you close on the purchase.

Let's go back to the beginning chapter. In 2005, I purchased 10 properties from builder at wholesale prices They were 20% below market value.

Purchase price: $150,000
Market value: $180,000
Down payment: $30,000 +$5,000 closing cost
Instant equity gain: $30,0000

I made 85% on our money as soon as I closed on them. These homes were new and were able to rent them out quickly and I turned around to refinance cash out all my initial capital without payment for any taxes. Remember, you do not pay taxes on the money that you get from a cash out refinance. You will pay taxes only on the equity you gain after the investment property is sold. This is relevant for your primary residence, second home, and investment properties.

Fast Closing
Another one of the great things about this type of purchase is that it closes quickly. Most of the time, the sale will close within seven to fourteen days.

They close quickly because the seller is generally having some type of personal issue and they need to get out of the house. They will be willing to sell the property for less, and they want to have money from the sale as quickly as possible. This can make getting into the real estate rental business fast and easy.

Hard Money Lending
To get this type of property, you will buy through the use of hard money lenders. The interest rate can be high, though. It is typically between 9% and 13%. However, the hard money lenders do not run your credit. They lend to you based solely on the fact that the property

is below market value (minimum 30%). These properties, as mentioned, are difficult to find when you first starting out, but they are worth looking for once you establish your comfort level of knowledge to venture your investment buying though this strategy.

If you have cash saving account that earn little interest, it's very good way to get a 20-35% return on your money yearly. You can buy one or two properties per year with the same amount of money, then flip them for quick gain and pay some ordinary income gain at your current year tax rate. This is income-generation strategy, but not wealth-building.

The best part of wealth-building strategy is using your Self-IRA account (it is a tax free retirement you should consult with our CPA or financial advisor how to set this up). Once it is set up, you use to buy wholesale properties with a discount 20-30% of purchase price. You can do a little update and then resale/flip those for quick cash, but you do not have to pay tax for the short-term capital gain. The gain will stay within your self-IRA account to reinvest for other projects. I have done a lot of this type of transactions in our self-IRA accounts. The return is exponential! Some years, I was able to double our money in every 18 months.

Bank-Owned Property (REO)/Foreclosure Properties

You can buy these wholesale properties though real estate agents who represent banks selling non-performing properties. This means they took back the properties of borrowers who could not make their payments on time. They wanted to sell these properties quickly because they do not want non-performing loans on their books, as it looks really bad for their bank credit rating. They offer a price discount to general public to sell quickly. Their job is collecting interest on your loan, not holding property to make a monthly cash flow. You will find a lot more buyers in this market because they are listed though MLS (Multiple Listing Service) property listing sites and all other well-known listing media. You can find the purchase price 7-10% below market value, but it's a very competitive market! You do not need to have a hard money loan to buy this type of property. The bank will have the same 30-45 day closing period to get your loan approval, just like the way you purchase investment property on a retail purchase.

Instant Equity Is KING in Real Estate Investment.

One of the reasons that I like this option the most is because after you purchase, you get instant equity in the home – generally between 7% and 30%. Imagine how nice it is to have that much equity in a home. It means you are that much closer to making your next purchase.

Why Does the Strategy Work?

Here's an example of how this will work in the real world so you can get an idea of what the strategy looks like in practice.

Home value: $300,000
Purchase price: $240,000
Rental income: $3000

You can already see what a good deal this can be. You've paid less for the property and you have the instant equity we mentioned. However, you do still need to do some work with properties like this to get them ready, as they are generally fixer-uppers. *Most of the wholesale properties do need some work after closing. You must know how much will be needed so you can be prepared with funds to make it ready for rent.*

Good for Properties Close to Home

This type of strategy works the best with homes that are in your hometown or that are within easy driving distance. Since they are generally going to need repairs, it means you will need to have a team of contractors that can work with you and get the property ready.

Once you have fixed up the property, you can start renting it out. However, you could also flip the property if you find that it would make more financial sense for you. This book is about building your wealth from rental properties, but if you see a good opportunity from a flip, it might be worth considering.

80% of my rental projects were purchased with discounts and this strategy alone was able to create true wealth in our net worth. I can assure you it does work well. You will need to attend local real estate networking events so you can meet up with those who sell wholesale properties. Most of them are very new in the business and you need to be selective about who you want to work with. They are the ones will bring you a lot of good below market value properties to flippers or to buy and hold investors. If you find five top wholesale investors in each market, your inbox will flood with properties for your review. You can cherry-pick the best investment to add to your portfolio. I receive at least 50-100 properties a month, but I only buy the best couple of them.

It takes some time and work to find these properties, but the investment is well worth it for you to venture out to build your wealth a lot sooner.

Buy Bulk from Your Local Bank

The third option is a good strategy for those who have been in the business for a while and who have the skills, as well as the funds, needed. If you are thinking about buying from the bank in bulk, you will want to get to know the asset manager. In addition, you need to start building connections with a number of others in the field. These include:

- Other investors
- Contractors
- Tradespeople
- Suppliers
- Real Estate CPA
- Real Estate Attorney
- Family Attorney
- Real Estate wholesalers
- Private lenders

How is this a good option? During the burst of the housing bubble, a number of smaller local banks needed to liquidate the homes that were in foreclosure and they needed to do it quickly. There are still a number of foreclosures available, and banks are trying to unload them. It is possible to find banks that still have a number of properties they would like to sell today. They aren't necessarily still from the housing crash, of course, but people still have properties they can't afford and foreclosures occur.

It is possible to buy up to three or even four properties at a time when banks are trying to liquidate the homes. You can often find some steep discounts on these homes because the banks are so desperate to get rid of them. The banks may even be willing to provide the mortgages for the homes for you, so that you will not need private money lenders. Sometimes they only need your down payment and they carry the mortgage loans for you once they access your investment background and credit.

In order to qualify to buy in bulk, you will need to have a good job and a good credit history. Later in the book, we'll talk about ways that you can improve your credit score so lenders do not see you as a risk.

If you happen to have the cash available, banks are often willing to offer an even larger discount.

Why Are the Banks So Quick to Sell the Properties?

The longer the banks hold the properties, the more money they are losing. They want to sell the homes so they can recoup some of their initial expenditure, and that's why they want to sell quickly and at big discounts. Banks lend money. They are not in the business of renting properties.

Since you will need to have some money available when you are investing in bulk properties through the banks, this might not be the best option for those who are just starting out in the rental business. However, as you start to get more properties and increase your wealth, this can be a very good way to increase the number of homes that you have available for rental in a very short time. You get an even better discount when you purchase the properties with cash. They're motivated to unload them to you to save their credit rating.

Owner Financing

Buying an owner-financed property could be a good option for you as well, but it will require quite a bit of legwork on your part. You will need to take the time to get out there and look for deals from owners who are willing to use this option. It's important that you understand exactly how this works.

What Is Owner Financing and How Does It Work?

Sometimes, you and the owner of a property might find it easier if they are the ones who offer the financing rather than the banks or another lender. In this case, the buyer, you, would finance the property directly through the seller. You would pay the seller each month rather than paying a bank. This can be helpful in many instances.

Those who are getting started and who do not have perfect credit can find it difficult to get approval for a loan through a traditional lender, even when they have a good down payment. Other times, the interest rates offered might be higher than what the buyer wants to pay. Enter owner financing. You can create an agreement with the seller.

In some cases, such as if they own the home free and clear, they will carry all of the financing. In other cases, they will carry part of the financing, so you do not have to get a massive loan.

Both the sellers and the buyers will benefit from this type of financing. Let's look at the benefits that each party gets.

Seller Benefits

- Higher sales price
- Tax breaks

- Monthly income (they get income from you each month, just as you would get money from your renters)
- Shorter listing term

Buyer Benefits

- Easier qualifications
- Tailored financing
- Flexible down payments
- Lower closing costs
- Take control of the property quickly

As you can see, there are a number of benefits for everyone with these types of sales. Of course, it isn't easy to find homeowners who are willing to act as the financer. You may find it easier if you approach homeowners who have had their properties listed for a long time without a sale. They may be more willing to make a deal because they are getting desperate to sell.

As long as there is nothing severely wrong with the property, and you are sure you can make money off of it from renting it out, then this could be a good option to pursue.

Bank-Owned Property (REO)

Another option to consider is bank-owned property or REO. The acronym REO stands for real estate owned, which simply means that it is a foreclosed property that is now owned by the bank or another lender. If the bank is the highest bidder at the foreclosure auction, or if there were no third-party bids at the auction, it means that the property goes back to the lender.

Lenders do not like to have these properties, as they are a liability to them. They want to sell them as quickly as possible. Thus far, this might sound quite a bit like buying properties wholesale from the bank, which we talked about earlier. There is a difference, though.

The biggest difference is the fact that the equity that you can get when you purchase these properties is going to be quite a bit lower than when you are buying from wholesalers and in bulk from the small, local banks.

In addition, when you buy through the bank, you can be sure that there is not a lien or other type of encumbrance on the property. It is an easy way to find properties that are often heavily discounted, since the banks want to get rid of them.

You will find quite a few other benefits as well, including:

- Lower risk
- Less competition
- The bank may be willing to pay closing costs
- The property is generally empty, so you do not have to go through the process of eviction.

Finding REOs

These types of properties are available to the general public, and you can find these homes in a number of different ways. You can search the internet for REOs, go directly to the local banks and ask them if they have any properties available, or you can work with an REO real estate specialist.

You will find that it's generally easier and less time-consuming to work with a specialist, as they know who to ask and where to go. There's a good chance that they already have some information on a couple of properties in the area that the bank wants to get rid of. You can call any real estate office in your areas and ask the front desk receptionist to give you a couple of agent names who specialize in REO. Some offices have REO specialists, some don't. But you can Google real estate offices and find out all the locations close to where you live. Once you get a few names, then you can set up a time to meet with them for coffee and share your interest about buying REO from them when they have REO listings available. I am sure that they like to work with investors who are ready to buy their listings even before they're on the market. You need to give them your specific criteria as far as what you're looking for in price range, the location of the property, etc. When you know precisely what you're looking for, it is much easier for you and the agent to work together, saving everyone's time!

What Strategy Is Best?

While I have had the most success with wholesale properties, each of these strategies has its place. You will need to look at your current financial situation, as well as your credit to determine which one will be the best choice for you.

CHAPTER 10:
PROPERTY INSPECTION IS A MUST

When you find a property that looks like it has an amazing price that you just can't beat, it's time to rein in your excitement. If it's a price that's too good to be true, well, it just might be too good to be true. The property may have quite a few problems that you aren't aware of.

Even when you visit the home and do a walkthrough, you will not necessarily find all of the problems unless you are an electrician, plumber, roofer, and a master craftsman. Chances are that you don't have all of these skills, so you need to find another way to determine what's wrong with the property and what the actual value is so you can be sure you aren't wasting your investment on a money pit.

Don't make the mistake of trusting the seller when they say that the property is in good condition. Sometimes, they want to get out of the house. Other times, they don't even know the house has issues. Saving a few hundred dollars on an inspection is not worth the headaches that you could face down the road if the property turns out to be a disaster.

Property inspection is a MUST.

Top Reasons to Get an Inspection

In this section, I am going to outline all of the major reasons that you will want to have an inspection on the property that you are considering buying.

- Safety
- Provides you with a way out
- Reveals illegal changes and additions
- Tool for negotiation
- Understand potential future costs
- Find the deal breakers
- See the property for what it is

Safety

First on the list is safety. The home inspector will look for things that could make the home dangerous to occupy. For example, they will look for issues with carbon monoxide and radon. They will also look for problems with toxic mold. Any of these issues could harm people who live there, including your renters.

If you have a property that wasn't properly inspected and you put your tenant's health in danger, it can come back to haunt you. Of course, you also don't want anyone to have to be in a potentially dangerous environment, even without the possibility of legal trouble coming into the picture.

The inspection will ensure that there aren't any dangers in the home that are lurking just beneath the surface. It's a good idea to have elements in your purchase contract that will allow you to cancel the offer to buy if hazards such as these are detected. In the following chapter, we'll talk more about these purchase contracts and what needs to go into them.

Provides You With a Way Out

This is one of the most important reasons to have a home inspection, and this is the reason I feel it is essential when you buy any property, even something that is relatively new and that *should* be in good condition. The inspection will provide you with all of the essential information you need when you are deciding whether to purchase a house or pass.

You will understand the costs and the type of maintenance the property will require. The inspection will give you the opportunity to pass on the house if you find that it is not suitable for you financially because of the repairs.

Reveals Illegal Changes and Additions

Something else that the home inspection will find is whether there have been any alterations or additions made to the home that happened without a proper permit. They can also find code violations on these new areas if there are any.

Think about the problems that an unapproved addition could cost. You aren't getting more out of the property if the addition has not gone through the proper channels because it affects so many different aspects of the property including the taxes, usability, insurance, and overall value of the home.

This means that you will later have to fix these issues so that they are in line with the code, or pay more on your taxes because of the additions. You need to know this information before buying.

Tool for Negotiation

When your inspector finds things wrong with the property, it doesn't automatically mean that you need to pass. If they are little things that you could fix on your own or with the help of an affordable contractor, then you might still want to buy the property.

In this case, the inspection will serve to help you in your negotiations. Let's say that the seller wants to get $300,000 for their property. However, your inspector finds some things that need to be fixed.

Maybe you need to replace the stairs to the basement. Perhaps there are some issues with the way the windows sit in the frames.

All of these little things are areas that you can use to help you in the negotiations. The sellers will be more willing to lower their price if you take the property as it is. Of course, they might also be willing to fix the issues before you buy. This could work out in your favor as well.

Understand the Potential Future Costs

One of the huge reasons that you need to have an inspection of the property is so you understand what future problems might arise based on the current condition of the home. This can provide you with the information you need to determine whether the future costs still make the property worth buying or not.

Locate the Deal Breakers

The inspection is also going to reveal the "deal breakers." These are issues that are going to be too problematic and costly to repair. Later in the chapter, we will talk more about the things that should make you cancel your purchase of the property.

See the Property for What It Is

The inspection reveals the flaws of the property. Many buyers, whether they are buying the home to live in or they are buying it as a rental property, fall in love with a house without really seeing what's going on with the house. They might like the layout or the fact that it comes with a pool. They have already confirmed in their own minds that they like the house and that it is worth buying.

The property inspection will help to remove those rose-colored glasses so you understand the good and the bad of the house. Ultimately, the inspection helps you make the right decision.

Dangers of No Inspection

Without a home inspection, *you have no idea what you are buying.* Would you buy a used vehicle without having a mechanic you trust look at it first? A home is an even larger investment, so you *need* to have a property inspector come and check the house for you.

If you don't, you could lose tens of thousands of dollars, or even hundreds of thousands in some cases! Spending a couple hundred dollars for the inspection now and understanding the pros and cons of the property is essential. This is true of all properties that you buy. Even if you feel that you are handy around the house and know what to look for, you *still* want to bring in a professional.

Finding an Inspector

Now you know how important it is to have a home inspector look at the property before you buy, but you are probably wondering how you can find a good inspector. Fortunately, it's not too difficult. You just need to do your homework. Sure, you could pick an inspector at random from the phone book or from a quick internet search. However, that's not going to provide you with the *best* inspector.

You can look online and in the phonebook to find inspectors. However, you can't hire them without a little more research. Trust me, when you put in the time to find a great inspector, you will be happy with the results. It can save you a substantial amount of money, not to mention headaches. You can also use them for all of the potential properties you are going to buy.

Of course, when you start to branch out into other locations in the state, or out of state, you need to make sure that you find inspectors for each of those areas as well.

Here are some of the most important things that you need to consider and ask when you are looking for a home inspector for the rental property you are considering purchasing.

- Can you be there for the inspection?
- Check out reviews
- Request a sample report
- Ask about the length of the inspection
- Are they part of a professional inspection group?
- Ask about experience
- Ask what is and is not included on the inspection
- Check the licenses

Can You Be There for the Inspection?

Inspectors should be more than happy to have you tag along on the inspection, and this is one of the first questions that you should ask. If they do not allow you to come on the inspection, then it could be a sign that they are not doing proper inspections. You don't *have* to go along on all of the inspections, but you should be allowed to attend them if you wish.

Going to an inspection will provide you with a good opportunity to learn more about the property you are thinking about buying, and you will get an idea of what repairs might be needed in real time. If the inspector is worth their salt, they will explain every step of the inspection and everything that they find along the way.

Check Out Reviews

Of course, in today's world, it is very easy to find reviews online for anything, and that includes home inspectors. When you start to look at inspectors, you will want to check out places such as Yelp! and Angie's List to find honest reviews written from customers about their home inspectors.

In addition, you can ask for references. However, with references, you need to realize that the inspector is cherry-picking and will send you to their clients that they know will provide them with a glowing review. That's why it is important to check out those aforementioned online review sites so you can get a look at some of the unbiased reviews.

Request a Sample Report

Ask if you can get a copy of a sample report. The reason you want to look at a sample report is so you can get an idea of how thorough they are and how clearly they write. Good reports need to talk about the problem and explain why it is an issue and what needs to be done to fix it. Clarity is important, since you will be using your own report when you are determining whether you want to buy the property or not.

The reports should include photos, as well, so you have a visual reference. Even if you go on the inspection with the inspector, you need to know that their report is going to be clear enough for you to understand later when you are talking with contractors to get estimates and trying to make your decision.

Ask About the Length of the Inspection

Most of the time, an inspection will take between two to three hours to complete. If the house is very small, it will take less time, and if it is large, it will take more time, naturally. If you find an inspector who says that he or she can be in and out of the house in an hour, steer clear. That's not enough time to perform a high-quality, thorough inspection of the property. It means they are cutting corners, and that's not something you can afford.

Are They Part of a Professional Inspection Group?

There are a number of professional inspector groups and organizations around the country, including ASHI (American Society of Home Inspectors) and NAHI (National Association of Home Inspectors).

Ideally, you want to make sure the home inspector you choose is part of at least one of these associations. This doesn't necessarily vouch for their quality. However, it does show that they have at least a certain level of training and professionalism.

Ask About Experience

In addition, you want to ask the inspector about their experience. How long have they been in business and how many inspections have they done? Where and how did they receive their training? Have they taken any special courses, and do they keep up with changes to the laws?

In general, you will find that it is better to choose someone who does home inspections as a full-time job rather than someone who does it in their spare time. That's not to say that some part-time inspectors can't do great jobs. It simply means that they generally don't have as much experience or as much time to commit to the task of inspections.

Ask What Is and Is Not Included on the Inspection

Make sure that you know what the inspection will cover and what it doesn't cover before hiring an inspector. In addition, ask if there are any special conditions that may prohibit them from checking certain areas. For example, in the dead of winter, it might not be possible to perform an inspection of the roof.

Licensed home inspectors are required to provide a written report that is delivered to their clients no later than a week after the inspection. It is preferable to receive the inspection report within 48 hours after the inspection, because you will have enough time to review details and time to call the specialist vendor to do a thorough check about the cost for specific repairs, like foundation, A/C, roof, or plumbing issues. You want to make sure that the repair costs will not add up to more on the top of the purchase price than you were expecting.

Never buy a property above market value!

Here is a list of the things that you can expect to find on an inspection report.

- Foundation and framing of the house
- Siding, balconies, walkways, driveways, railings

- Roof, including shingles, flashing, and skylights
- Electrical system
- Plumbing system
- Heating system
- Cooling system
- Interior features, including walls, floors, ceilings, doors, stairs, railings, and windows
- Insulation
- Ventilation
- Fireplaces, chimneys, and vents

However, it is important to remember that a home inspection is only a visual inspection. This means that certain things such as septic systems and underground pipes are not able to be inspected.

The following are some of the things that you will not find on a basic home inspection report.

- Swimming pools
- Hot tubs
- Kitchen appliances
- Lawn sprinkler systems
- Home alarms
- Detached structures
- Well systems
- Termites

However, even though these things might not be included in a "basic" inspection, you can find many inspectors who can inspect these different areas of the home. You simply need to make sure they are qualified to conduct these types of inspections. Since they cover additional areas, it could cost more for the inspection. It's wise to do them, even with more costs. Inspection costs are usually much cheaper compared to the real actual repair costs.

Check the Licenses

Many states require that home inspectors have licenses. Check to see the rules in your state, and in any states where you plan to buy property. If they require a license, ask if you can get a copy of their license as well as their insurance. This will provide you with the peace of mind you need to determine whether you are working with someone who is able to do a good job on the inspection, and to know that there is coverage in case they mess something up!

What Should Make You Cancel the Purchase?

In some cases, the inspection will show you that the property needs to have a substantial amount of work before it is actually viable for renters to live in. If it needs only superficial work and repairs that are relatively easy to fix without costing a fortune, it might still be worthwhile to get the property.

However, when the problems are more severe, it will become too expensive and too much of a hassle to buy. The following are some of the biggest reasons you will want to pass on a piece of property after an inspection reveals the flaws.

- Foundation problems
- Major AC and heating issues
- Roof needs replacement
- Major plumbing issues

Problems with the foundation can be extremely expensive to fix. In some cases, the home might require an entirely new foundation. This is far too much to pay for on top of buying the home.

If there is central air conditioning and heating that no longer work, it may cost too much to replace or repair. Some repairs for the AC and heating might be minor, but they could indicate other issues with the home.

Even if the owners are willing to reduce the price of the home, they aren't likely to reduce it enough to make it a good purchase. In addition, you have to think about how long it would take to redo the foundation or the roof. Remember that the goal of these types of properties is for an investment that will start making you money as soon as possible. If you have to wait months and months before you can rent it out, you will be bleeding money. When you start out, you want to avoid some of these major updates; you can eventually deal with these updates when you have established a trusted network of trade vendors in the areas where you invest. As for me, at this point these become little issues because I have established my trusted network of trade vendors so I can still make the transactions work, based on how much of a discount the seller is willing to give to compensate me for my investment of time and money. I have also found that I made more return with even deeper discount in price because a lot of investors do not want to deal with these problems. I have less competition and more price discount with sellers.

What Does the Inspection Report Say?

You've taken the time to make sure that you have a high-quality inspector looking over the home you are thinking about buying. You attended the inspection and now you have the report sitting in front of you.

What's the verdict?

At this point, it is time to start looking at the pros and cons of the property. Does it need to have some large repairs, such as the deal breakers we talked about earlier? If so, then you should simply avoid the property. Simple as that.

However, if there are some other issues with the home that are relatively minor, or at least they seem minor, it is time to do a little research to get a better understanding of what you will have to do to make those repairs.

You might want to get in touch with a contractor who can provide you with an estimate of what it would cost to get those areas of the home in shape. Keep in mind that they will be providing only rough estimates, and the end cost could be much more.

Run the numbers and see whether it still makes sense to buy the property or not. Don't rush into a decision, and you will find that you are far more successful when buying rental real estate.

CHAPTER 11:
WHAT TO PUT IN THE PURCHASE CONTRACTS

You do not want to get stuck with a property that has major problems, and you certainly do not want to lose your deposit. How can you guarantee that this type of nightmare situation doesn't happen to you? What you need to do is create a purchase contract, also called a purchase agreement.

What Is a Purchase Contract?

When you find a property that you would like to buy, you will provide the owner with an offer to purchase the home. This is the purchase contract, and they tend to be very short and basic. The contract helps to open up negotiations, and the clauses in the contract can make sure that you don't lose your deposit and that you are not stuck with a piece of property that you do not really want.

What Needs to Be in the Purchase Contract?

However, just because it is basic, that doesn't mean that it shouldn't keep you protected. In many states, the real estate agent will have a standard purchase offer. You can still request that they make changes to the contract to meet your needs, though.

Other states require that you have an attorney in a real estate transaction. Some of these states include New York, North Carolina, and Alabama. You can request additional clauses for the purchase contract through the attorney as well.

Let's look at some of the most important clauses that you *need* to have in the contract in order to keep yourself safe.

- Inspection period and contingency clause
- Property address and legal description
- Walkthrough inspection clause
- Amount of down payment
- Mortgage contingency provision
- Length of the offer
- Closing date and take-possession date
- Items included and not included in the sale
- Who holds the earnest money?
- Seller guarantee
- Clause that requires return of earnest money deposit

Inspection Period and Contingency Clause

The purchase contract needs to have an inspection and contingency clause. This essentially means that you have the right to inspect the property and determine whether you want to go ahead with the purchase or not.

For example, if you discover that the roof of the home is going to need replacement, which would be something that you didn't know at the time of making the initial offer, you would be able to pull out of the purchase.

If you are purchasing a piece of property that's in your own back yard, then you should request a minimum of seven business days from the inspection to cancel. If you are making a purchase outside of the state, you should request a period of ten business days.

Refer to the last chapter when it comes to the things that you need to look for on your inspection report to determine whether it is in your best interest to cancel the purchase of the property.

Property Address and Legal Description

It is important that you make sure that any contracts and agreements in a real estate purchase have a legal description of the property along with the address. The legal description of the property doesn't include the buildings. Rather, it includes the boundaries of the property.

Walkthrough Inspection Clause

Adding a walkthrough inspection clause can be a good idea as well. This ensures that you can do a walkthrough a day or two before the closing date to ensure that everything is good to go and that the seller has lived up to whatever agreements they may have made in the contract.

For example, it ensures that the place is reasonably clean, the seller hasn't taken property that was supposed to remain, and that they have moved out entirely. This simply ensures that you don't run into any issues when it is time to take possession of the property.

Amount of Down Payment

This one's simple. It documents the amount of the down payment that you have put toward the house. This protects you during the purchase, if you need to get your deposit back for some reason.

In addition, the contract should include the entire amount you are offering for the property.

Mortgage Contingency Provision

This provision should be in the contract as well. It simply states that you can be released from the offer if for some reason you are not able to get a loan at a specified interest rate within a specific period – generally between 45 and 60 days. Some sellers do not want to wait for this long for a mortgage contingency. Your offer is weaker when there are more buyers for the same property. To stay competitive with other buyers, you should have done preapproval in advance before making a purchase offer. Also when you work with agents, they're motivated to help you more when they know you're a qualified buyer. No business professional wants to waste time.

Length of the Offer

Since this is generally used to open up negotiations, you will also want to let them know how long the offer will remain on the table. You could limit the seller to 48 hours to make a decision on whether they want to sell or not. This can keep the seller from prolonging the process and waiting for other bids to come in from potential buyers.

Closing Date and Take-Possession Date

This is rather standard. When will the date of closing be and when will you actually take possession of the property? This information should be in the contract. In some cases, the seller might actually need to stay in the house after the closing date, and you may need to rent to them on a short-term basis while they purchase another home. This is not always the case, but it could come up. 45-60 days closing is standard, and some can even close on/before 30 days when the property is already vacant.

Items Included and Not Included
in the Sale

What items will be included in the purchase of the home? For example, some people may include appliances such as the oven and the refrigerator, or certain lighting fixtures. Get in writing what they will include in the purchase price and what they will be taking with them. When you do your walkthrough inspection, you can make sure that they have abided by the information in the contract.

Who Holds the Earnest Money?

When the home is waiting to close, you need to know who will be holding the deposit money, also called the earnest money. Most of the time this is going to be a title company with assigned escrow agent for your transaction, but you will want to have their information in the contract.

Seller Guarantee

The seller guarantee is to ensure that they are providing you with a clear title to the home that doesn't have a lien or any other issues tied up with it. They are generally going to provide you with a certificate of title, a title insurance policy, or an abstract of title. The title company is the company the seller pays to provide the title insurance policy for buyers and they will make sure the title is clear when it is transferred to you. Sometimes the title insurance can be paid for by buyer, based on the purchase agreement.

Clause That Requires Return of Earnest Money Deposit

You should also have a clause in the contract that is very clear about what happens in the event that the sale is not completed based on certain contingencies that you can detail in the contract. This is to ensure that you receive a return of your down payment money.

For example, you are buying the property on the contingency that it will pass the inspection. However, if the inspection reveals that the foundation of the house is in terrible condition, it's not a property you are going to want to buy. This clause allows you to have your down payment returned and you will be able to walk away from the deal without losing anything other than some time.

How Long Should the Purchase Contract Be?

One of the mistakes that some new investors make is that they create purchase contracts that are a dozen pages long and that have a lot of confusing legal jargon in them. When you are coming up with the contract, try to keep it as short as possible while including all of the needed information and contingencies.

Work with an attorney to draft the contract, but make sure that it the language is easy enough for laymen to understand. If a seller sees a massive purchase contract that they will need to decipher and that has a lot of legal terms and contingencies they do not understand or that they are not comfortable with, they may just decide that selling the house to you would be too much of a hassle.

Just make sure that the purchase contract has the essentials we talked about here, and speak with your attorney about any other items that might be a good idea based on the individual sale.

Every state has different set of law and regulations to follow; it's crucial to read the buy/sell contract agreement for the state before you're going to make a purchase. It is even better to hire a local real estate attorney to explain it all to you in layman's terms so you get to understand about it better. You want to become an informed investor and build up your level of confidence. It's better to learn early and avoid some costly mistakes in the future

CHAPTER 12:
HOW TO BUY REAL ESTATE OUTSIDE OF YOUR HOMETOWN

Earlier, I said that it was a good idea to make your first real estate investments for rentals in your own hometown, and I stand by that. However, you will eventually want to make your way out of the back yard and start to see what other cities in your state, and what other states, have to offer.

In order to do this, you need to make sure you are willing to do plenty of research to ensure you are making the right decision. *It takes a bit MORE work, and you need to be willing to delegate a number of tasks since you aren't in the area all the time.* However, once you get started, you will discover it's not quite as difficult as you might have thought.

Let's look at all of the things you will need to do in order to invest in real estate in another state the right way.

- Research using the web
- Visit the area or at least two weeks
- Build your professional team

Research Using the Web

Just as when you were researching your own hometown to determine whether it would be a good place for your investment, you need to make sure you do the same when you invest out of town. In fact, you need to put in even more work and research since you likely know little to nothing about the area you are considering.

You need to research all of the elements that we mentioned in Chapter 4 to determine whether it is in your best interest to buy a home in the area. From there, you can start to look for potential properties, but you never want to take action until you have completed the following two steps.

Visit the Area for at Least Two Weeks

You need to have "boots on the ground" in the area where you want to invest. This will give you a much better idea about the city and the different neighborhoods and locations. This is essential when you are going to be investing.

When you visit certain areas, you can see firsthand whether it looks like a safe neighborhood or not. You can see what amenities are in the area and what it might be like to live there permanently. During this trip, after you meet with your chosen real estate agent, then you must go around as many areas as the agent can show you, and then you can map down the areas of the city where you would potentially like to focus on buying rental properties.

It is important that you treat this like a working vacation, though. You aren't taking a trip just to enjoy the scenery in a new city. You need to make sure that you are putting your investment money to good use, and seeing things for yourself is one of the best ways to do it. You can put your research to the test.

Of course, you are going to need to have some people who can help you out with the process of buying and managing a property. You can start to build your team while you are on your two-week visit.

You must gather all the research in advance before making your first trip to this city after you know the return on investments make sense, and the return on your money could cover paying for the real estate professional team running these investment properties for you.

Build Your Professional Team

You need to have a team of pros who can help you with every step of the process from finding a home to buying and managing it. Before you take off for your visit, you will want to research each of the following to help make your search easier.

- Real estate agent
- Loan officer
- Property management company
- Real estate attorney
- Contractors

Real Estate Agent

You do not want to choose just any real estate agent to help you find properties that might make good investments. You need to choose a professional real estate agent who has been working in the city for at least five years.

You can find agents by searching sites such as Zillow.com and Realtor.com. Make a list of at least five agents and then interview them. You could conduct interviews with them over the phone, and then choose the three best to meet with when you are on your trip to the city.

When you interview them, make sure that you ask at least these four questions (in addition to any others that you might have).

- Have you worked with out-of-state investors before?
- Do you work with several knowledgeable mortgage brokers, who specialize in funding mortgages for real estate investors?
- How many out-of-state real estate investors have you successfully helped in the past?
- Are you specialized in REO (Real estate owned) properties?
- Can you give me three real estate investor referrals so I can learn more about you and what you offer?
- How long have you been in the business?
- Are you real estate investor yourself?

When you meet with them during your two-week trip, you will be able to learn more about them and how they conduct business. You will also be getting a better idea of what is available for you in the city in terms of good property rentals.

How to select which agent to work with

It's better to work with agent who is real estate investor themselves. They are wearing the investor hat so they do understand the bottom line of the investment is making money. An agent who specializes in REO properties is a plus because you can purchase properties with some discount so that you can build instant equity after purchase. The agent also has worked extensively with outside state investors so they already know what to expect with a long-distance transaction (time delay, inspection urgency). And you need someone who has been in the real estate business for at least years.

Mortgage Broker/Bank Loan Officer

In addition to a real estate agent, you will want to look for a lender who has experience working with people in your situation. Namely, you need to find someone who has experience when it comes to working with rental residential loans.

Just as you did with the real estate agent, you will want to take the time to research loan officers before you head to the city. Make a list of several questions that you can talk with to get an idea of their experience when it comes to working with rental residential property loans. Meet with several when you are on your trip and then you can make your decision.

You can get a couple of referral names from real estate agents that you selected. Usually they know how they work together so the purchase transaction can move to closing table smoothly. I preferred working with mortgage brokers because they have wide selection of loan options available to investors/consumers; usually they have up to 500 different loan options. They work with multiple wholesale lenders/banks. Each bank can give them at least 20 loan options. If they're an approved broker with 20 wholesale lenders, then they have 400 loan options available to offer to any borrowers. A bank direct loan officer has limited loan options because each bank can offer about 15-20 loan options. The closing costs are the same whether you use mortgage broker or direct bank loan officer. Once your real estate business is established, you want a lot of options when it comes to financing your investment properties. Your money is moving around between projects, which is very critical in real estate. You want to be prepared to have more options when the opportunity comes.

The key is making sure the mortgage broker/bank loan agent has extensive experience in loan approval for real estate investors, and that they know the streamlined process involved with rental properties.

Property Management Company

A property management company can be a real lifesaver when you have out-of-state properties. They take care of the duties of the landlord for you and they can provide you with peace of mind in regard to your property. However, you need to make sure that you choose the right company for the job.

Let's look at some of the different duties that the property management company will be able to handle for you and the benefits they can offer.

- Saving time and preventing frustration
- Collecting rent
- Taking care of maintenance
- Taking care of repairs
- Dealing with tenant problems and complaints
- Marketing to find tenants
- Dealing with evictions

As you can see, they can make your life quite a bit easier. Essentially, all you need to do is reap the rewards of having a rental property. Of course, you need to make sure that you are choosing the best property management company for the job.

Some of the questions that you need to ask include:

- How long they have been in business? (You want to choose a company that has been in the field for at least five years.)
- Have they worked with out-of-state investors in the past?
- How many people do they have on staff to manage the properties?
- How many properties do they manage?
- Do they work with in-house handymen or contractors?
- Do they charge the service fee on top of the repair cost?
- What is the monthly management service fee?
- How often do they inspect the property?
- How do they screen tenants?
- Can you get involved with the tenant screening process?
- Are they in good standing with BBB?
- Can they provide you a few out-of-state investor references who are still actively working with them?

You can do phone interviews with at least four property management companies and then compare to see which one can perform the job best. Chapter 16 will go deeper on how to select a good management company to represent you in running your real estate business.

Real Estate Attorney

It is crucial to pay for a real estate attorney phone consultation about the state that you're going to invest in. What are the things that you should look for when buying property in that state? What are the important items that you need to put in the purchase contracts besides what we have covered in previous chapters?

Contractors

In many cases, you will be buying a property that might need to have a little work done on it before it is in good shape to become a rental. This means you need to have contractors that you can trust. Just as you would research contractors in your area for your local properties, you need to so the same thing when you are looking at out-of-state contractors.

You should have a number of different contractors researched and vetted that you can call on when you need them. If the property management company has contractors they've worked with in the past, they can refer you to them.

You need to look for the following contractors, even if you don't need to hire all of them. Simply having their names and numbers ready to go in the event that you do need their services will give you peace of mind.

- Plumber
- Roofer
- AC and heating
- Electrician
- Handyman

Depending on the property, you might find that you may want to have some other contractors on call as well, such as a landscaping crew. Having professional landscapers does cost extra, but if the property has a large yard and you want to make sure it is maintained properly, this could be a good option. Just have them come to the property twice a month to maintain it.

The goal is to find an agent, loan officer, property management company, real estate attorney, and contractor who make you feel comfortable and whom you can use for all of your investments in the city. Take your time so you can be happy with your decisions.

Be prepared that you may change property management company a few times until you will find ones who can take pride in managing your investments and also care for you by minimizing your expenses and maximizing your return.

Visit my website to get a link to select the three best companies to work with you.

http://korianne.com/resources/

Summary of the Buying Process

Okay, I thought it would be a good idea to add a quick summary of the things that we've covered and learned so far. This following list distills the information into short and easy-to-learn chunks.

- Select a market that's in your back yard as your first rental property investment and then start investing in properties outside of the home area, as long as the return makes sense.

- Make an offer on the home after you have done the research and found the true value.

- Have a professional conduct a property inspection so they can determine if there is anything wrong with the property, which can help you in negotiations or save you from buying a money pit.

- Get the loan to maximize your return on investment, or ROI.

- Close on the property and take possession.

- Determine whether you want to manage the property on your own or if you want to hire a property management company. If you have just one property in your hometown, you may be able to handle the management on your own. However, if you have multiple properties or out-of-town properties, working with a property manager might be a better option.

- Have your exit strategy. Is it better for you to hold onto the property long-term or do a 1031 exchange? This exchange is able to provide an exception, and it will allow you to postpone paying tax on the gain, as long as you reinvest in a similar property as a part of the exchange. I will go over this in detail later in the book.

Wait Until You Are Ready

It can be quite tempting to try to invest in out of town and out-of-state properties, but as you can see, it takes some added work and research. Until you are comfortable with investing in your own hometown, you should avoid out-of-town investments. When you are ready, take things one step at a time.

Once you have invested in a few out-of-town properties, it will become second nature and you can expand your rental property business. Just make sure to surround yourself with a solid team.

PART 3:

How to Finance Your Rental and
Maximize Your Bottom Line Return

CHAPTER 13:
FINANCE YOUR RENTAL

Now, it is time that you figure out how you are going to finance your rental properties. When you are first getting your initial rental property, you will go through a process just as you would to buy a home that you would live in yourself. Remember that good credit is important if you want to have a good mortgage with a low rate. In the next chapter, we'll talk about how you can get your credit in order.

You need to know how much house you can afford for your rental investment. We've already talked about what I feel is the best option: single-family homes. You will need to have a good down payment on the property. *Try for at least 20%.* So, if you find a property that costs $300k, you would want to have a down payment of $60,000 and closing costs estimated at $4,000-6,000.

You should also make sure that you have money on hand for the closing costs. In some cases, the seller may agree to pay for the closing costs, but this is not something on which you should rely.

When you are getting a mortgage, you want to get a low interest rate, naturally. Try to get prequalified for a mortgage before you start looking at properties too closely. This will ensure that you know the amount you can actually afford, and it can make searching for the right property much easier. When you have been preapproved, it also shows the sellers that you are seriously interested in making a purchase.

You also need to work with a good real estate agent who can help you find properties in your area. Again, you want to make sure that the agent has experience working in the area for at least five years or so, and that they have worked with residential rental investors.

Once you have your financing in order and the loan will give you a good ROI, follow the rest of the steps we've covered – find a property, make an offer, get an inspection, buy the property and get it ready to rent.

Leverage the Bank Money to Create Wealth

You are also able to leverage your bank's money to create wealth. Here is an example:

Property purchase price: $300,000
Down payment: $60,000+ $5,000 closing cost
Loan amount: $240,000
Appreciation: 3% per year
Cash flow per year: $350x12/month = $4,200

The appreciation gains of the property ($300000 x 3%) = $9,000

Cash on cash return = $4,200/$65,000 down +closing cost = 6.4%

Return on investment (ROI): $9,000 (appreciation) + $4,200 (cash flow)
Total: $13,200

ROI = $13,200/$65,000 (down payment+closing cost)

ROI: 20.3%

Above is a quick example to analyze a purchase. You can access the resource page though my website to get the link for the investment property analysis tool.

http://korianne.com/resources/

When you start to make money on your home, and when you start to build equity in the home, it becomes easier to use that money to start buying more properties, as it is often easier to get another loan. The banks will see you as being more trustworthy, and they will be more willing to put up their money for a loan.

Should You Refinance When the Property Value Rises in a Few Years?

One of the big questions that many people have when they have had their first rental property for a few years is whether they should refinance. Let's say that the purchase price of the property was $300,000 and it is now valued at $400,000. That's a nice increase.

However, it is advisable to refinance only if you are going to do it so you can buy another property, which will help you to build your wealth faster. If you are in this situation, make sure that the refinancing will keep the new monthly mortgage price at the same level or a lower level, so that the rental income is still able to produce a positive monthly cash flow.

CHAPTER 14:
HOW TO BUILD A
GOOD CREDIT SCORE

Credit scores are the bane of many would-be investors out there. Most people understand that if they want to get a good interest rate on their mortgage, they need to have a good credit score. However, that's not always an easy thing to maintain. Perhaps you have had some trouble with your credit in the past. What should you do?

You need to repair your credit. It takes time, but it is something that you can actively work on right now. A *good* credit score is going to be 700, but you want to get it higher if you can.

Improve Your Credit Score First

Sure, it's exciting to think about having a rental property, and you are probably eager to get out there and buy your first rental home so you can start growing your wealth. Slow down for a minute and think about your credit score first.

It is very important that you take the time to improve your credit score *before* you try to get a loan for a piece of property, even if you have a large down payment. Even if the interest rate is only slightly higher, it can end up costing you many thousands of dollars over the course of the loan.

Throughout the rest of the chapter, I will share with you some simple things that you can do to help improve your credit score. If you have less-than-perfect credit, start working on repairing it right now so you can get into the business sooner.

- Check your credit and dispute errors
- Pay your bills on time
- Keep balances low
- Pay off debt

Check Your Credit and Dispute Errors

Sometimes, having bad credit really isn't your fault. There could be errors on your credit that are dragging you down. They will typically fall into one of three different categories.

- Identity errors
- Incorrect account details
- Fraudulent accounts

Identity Errors

The three main credit bureaus (TransUnion, Experian, and Equifax) each maintain their own consumer database that includes account info, payment history, and personal information. In some cases, one or more of these bureaus will have some of your information incorrect.

Many times, they are small errors, such as an incorrect address. However, they have the potential to be more problematic. If your name happens to be mixed up with someone else's name, it could affect your credit, as you will start to see *their* accounts on your report.

Incorrect Account Details

In some cases, the lender that provides the information to the credit reporting bureaus provides erroneous information. They might show the wrong limit on your credit card or they could show the wrong origin date of a loan that you have.

Fraudulent Accounts

Unfortunately, identity theft is becoming a real problem. When people use your name, Social Security Number, and other personal information to take out credit cards, then it is going to affect your credit. People who steal information like this are certainly not going to pay the bills, and the blame (as well as the bad credit) will fall to you.

You should check your credit report once per year, and you should scour it for anything that looks wrong or out of place. Notify the credit bureau of errors and possible identity theft if you find evidence.

Make sure that you place a security freeze on the account. This will ensure that they are not able to open up any more accounts in your name. Of course, you will not be able to open up a new line of credit at this time either. When the security freeze is in place, you will take care of the identity theft problem and try to get things righted with your credit.

Pay Your Bills on Time

This is one of the things that gets most people in trouble with credit. They don't pay their bills on time, and whenever you have late charges or collections in your name, it will have a drastic negative impact on your credit. This is *the most important* part of building or restoring good credit.

If you have trouble paying your credit card bills and other loans on time now, imagine how much worse it would be if you had an additional mortgage to consider! You have to get organized and make sure that you have a schedule for paying your bills that you adhere to each month.

Keep Balances Low

You must also strive to keep your balances low, and not have a revolving door of credit. Many people start spending on their credit cards as soon as they get them paid off. You should use credit cards only for necessary purchases, and you should make sure that you pay them on time, as mentioned, and that you keep the balances as close to zero as possible. This doesn't mean that you can never use your credit cards. It just means that you need to be smart about using them, and you need to pay them down as quickly as you possibly can.

Pay Off Debt

Work to pay off as much debt as you can. If you have a car payment, try to pay off the car. If you have high credit card balances, don't pay just the minimum each month. You are losing far too much money to interest when you do this.

If you have to, you can cut some of your current unnecessary expenses to pay down your debt faster. For example, cut back on going out to eat and start making coffee at home rather than buying it at an overpriced coffee shop each day.

Let's look at the amount of money that you are spending on coffee as an example. Let's say that you and your spouse each spend $4 a day for a cup of coffee during the week. In one week, you've spent $40 together. In a month, you've spent $160. Wouldn't that $160 be better served paying off some of your credit cards?

Looking for little ways to save here and there so you have more money to pay the bills can help you get your debt down much faster than you might have imagined. Once you have paid off the debt, you can put that extra money that you have each month into the down payment on a piece of property, for example.

Don't worry--once you start investing in property and building your wealth, you will find that you have plenty of money for overpriced coffee! For now, you need to think about the future, and that means you need to improve your credit score and make a few sacrifices here and there.

There Is No Quick Fix

Perhaps the most important lesson to take away from this chapter is that there is no quick fix to your credit score woes--no matter what you might hear from online companies promising to boost your credit score in two weeks or thirty days or whatever they claim.

It takes time for your credit score to go up, and you have to be patient. However, if you follow the simple advice in this chapter, you can be sure that it *will* go up.

Though it takes time, it doesn't mean that you have to be idle when it comes to your dream of starting a rental property business. In fact, now is the best time to do your research.

Keep Busy

While you are waiting and working on your credit score, that is the perfect time to start looking at potential areas of your city in which to invest. You can learn more about real estate in your state. You can learn how to complete some simple DIY repairs so you don't have to rely on hiring people to make fixes to the property.

Start learning more about the real estate agents in your area and how they operate. Keep an eye on the rental prices and watch the news to learn of any new industries that might be coming to the area and that could spur growth. Now is the time to learn, so that when your credit score is back in good shape you will be ready to go.

Add More to the Down Payment

You can also start to save more for your down payment. Once you have all of your other debt paid off, it will be easier to put aside added money for a down payment. Even if you are able to add only another $5000, it can make a big difference, and it might make it even easier to get a loan.

Let's say that you want to buy a property that's $300,000 and you've managed to save $60,000 for a down payment already. Adding another $5,000 or $10,000 to the down payment might not seem like much, but it really is. It means you will be able to take out a smaller loan. It also means that since the loan is smaller, there will be less overall interest to pay. Over the life of the loan, this will equate to savings.

Take your time and really work hard on your credit. It will make all the difference in the world when it comes to getting a mortgage and getting one at a good interest rate.

PART 4:

Property Management

CHAPTER 15:
MANAGING YOUR RENTAL
ON YOUR OWN

We've already talked a bit about what it will entail when you have your properties in your hometown or that are just as short drive away. While some of this is familiar territory (or at least it should be by now), in this chapter, I thought we'd go into a bit more detail so you have a better understanding of what you need to do to become a good landlord and manage your own property.

Committing these tips to memory is important, as they will make running your properties much easier.

- Things to look for when screening your tenants
- Building your home team
- Putting it in writing
- Respect
- Inspecting the property
- Making prompt repairs

Things to Look for When Screening Your Tenants

There's no such thing as putting too much emphasis on choosing the right tenants for your property! That's why I've talked about it several times in this book already, and why it is something that you need to take to heart. The wrong tenants can make being a landlord feel like a nightmare. **_Put in the time and work to find good tenants._** I promise you that it is well worth it. You can return to Chapter 6 for a refresher and resource page for links to the tenant screening and background check services. You must use this service to screen tenants.

Here, I want to talk about the most important elements for you to consider during your tenant screening.

- Job history
- Rental history
- Credit history

Job History

You might be wondering why a person's job history might be important. Well, it will show you a couple of different things. It shows you how long they've been at the same job and it shows you that they have an income to pay your rent. If they are the type of person who doesn't hold a job for more than a few months or even a year before needing to find another job for whatever reason, it could mean that they are not always going to have a job while they are living in your rental property. How are they going to pay rent if that happens?

Switching jobs doesn't always mean the tenant isn't worthwhile, but it is something that you will want to consider when you are deciding on the tenants.

Rental History

This is important as well. It gives you a good idea of how long the tenants tend to stay in one spot. You want to have as little vacant time in your property as possible, and if a tenant always moves as soon as their lease is up, they might not be the best choice if you are looking for someone who will be with you long-term. In addition, you can use their rental history to see if they've had any evictions.

Normally, you want to steer clear of people who have had recent evictions, but if everything else on their application looks good and checks out, you might still want to talk with them. Perhaps they fell on hard times and lost a job for a few months before getting back on their feet. You still want to be cautious, but it doesn't mean that everyone who has been evicted in the past is a bad person or that they will be a bad tenant. Sometimes, bad things just happen.

If you believe the risk is low enough, you may still want to rent to them. However, you may want to use a shorter-term lease, such as six months rather than a year-long lease, just in case they aren't paying on time.

Credit History

Always run a credit check on the people you are considering as your tenants. This will let you know how they take care of their finances. If you see that they have an abysmally low credit score because they are bad at making payments on time, you can be relatively sure that they will eventually fall behind on rent due to money mismanagement. Most of the time, you want to stay away from tenants that have a bad credit history just to be on the safe side.

In fact, you always want to err on the side of safety. Your mission is to look for the ideal tenants. They are out there. Double check on their monthly debts that they're supposed to pay, and make sure that with the monthly debts, their expenses do not exceed your rental payment, because if they do, then the tenants will likely to pay your rent late.

For example: If the tenant's monthly income is $4,000/mo before tax
After tax income (at 20% tax bracket): $3,200
Rent expense: $1,200/mo
Monthly debt payment: $1,500

Total expenses from the two above: $2,700/$3,200

Total expense is 84.4%

After the tenant pays the rent and monthly debt expenses, the leftover is $500/mo. Will this amount be enough for her to pay for food, insurance, utilities, gas? Maybe not; potentially the tenants will be late on their rent payment in the future. The risk to approve the tenants is high. *Make sure you factor in all the payments that the tenant is responsible for making monthly before approval. You can access all the monthly total payments by careful review of the tenant's credit report, or you can ask the property manager who manages your property.*

In addition to checking the job, rental, and credit history of your tenants, you also want to consider their criminal background. Again, you can go back to Chapter 6 to refresh your memory on checking criminal backgrounds.

You Can Always Use a Tenant Screening Service

Maybe you don't have the time or the resources available to perform all of these checks on your own. When you are starting out with your first property, this is entirely understandable. However, remember that you don't have to perform the screening on your own. You can use websites to run screenings, and even hire companies to do them for you. It's faster and easier. They provide you with the information you need, and then you can make your choice.

In Chapter 6, we also have a list of different tenant screening companies that you can consider using if you need some additional help finding the right tenants for your property.

Build Your Home Team

Even though you will be responsible for taking care of your property when it's in your hometown, that doesn't mean that you need to do everything alone. You will want to have a home team that you can rely on for certain things.

In addition to having a real estate agent to help you find great properties, you also need to have different types of contractors, as well as a handyman or handywoman who can take care of repairs and maintenance, an attorney in the event that you need to go through the eviction process, and someone to ensure you are doing your taxes correctly.

Put It in Writing

It is always important to create a rental agreement. These agreements will specify all of the important rental terms that the renter needs to know when they start renting the property. It also needs to include the names of the tenants residing in the property, the length of the lease, the amount of rent, whether they can have pets in the property, a no smoking indoors clause if you don't want the tenants to smoke inside, and the amount of the security deposit.

In addition, it should have information letting the tenant know who is responsible for certain types of maintenance or repairs. For example, if there is a minor repair, will the tenant or the landlord be responsible?

The agreement should also include when the rent is due, the late fees, whether there is a grace period or not, and what form of payment you take – check, money order, etc.

You can find some premade forms online, and they might be all you need for your rental agreement. However, I encourage you to read through any of these premade forms carefully to make sure that they include all of the information that you need. You may be able to amend some forms to make them work for you, or you might find it easier to have an attorney create an agreement that you can use for your properties.

The goal of this agreement is to provide the guidelines that the tenant needs to know and understand when they move into the unit. Keep in mind that when they read over the document, they may have some questions, or they may ask if you can amend part of the agreement.

For example, when you put in the policy for no pets, you might have been thinking about cats and dogs. Perhaps the tenant has a turtle or a goldfish that they would like to have with them. If you don't have a problem with that, then you can amend the agreement.

Respect

One of the mistakes that a small number of new landlords make, which gives a bad name to all landlords, is not treating their tenants with proper respect. It doesn't matter if you like the tenants or not; as long as they are paying their rent and are not doing anything to damage the property or to disturb the neighbors, you can't let any personal feelings affect the way you conduct business. That means that everyone is deserving of your respect.

Just because you happen to own rental property doesn't make you better than another human being, and you shouldn't act as though it does. When you treat each tenant with dignity and respect during all of your interactions, it will help you in your success.

Let's look at it from the perspective of a brand-new tenant who is looking to rent one of your properties. They are going to do the same thing that you do when you are looking for contractors or attorneys – they are going to look up information about you. If you have tenants whom you've treated poorly, you can be sure they will be leaving you and your properties bad reviews online.

All you have to do is be nice (not a *pushover*, simply *respectful*), and it will be much better for you in the end. Be fair and be respectful, but make sure that you require that the tenants abide by all of the rules in the tenancy agreement that you created.

Inspecting the Property

We talked about the benefits of having a rental property that is essentially in your own back yard. One of those is the fact that you are always nearby so you can conduct inspections of the property regularly. This doesn't mean that you have to set up a weekly schedule with your tenants so you can do a walkthrough – they would get sick of that as fast as you would. However, it does mean that you should to a walkthrough at least every six months or so.

One of the things that you need to remember about doing inspections on the property though is that you can't simply show up unannounced. As we mentioned before, you need to provide them with plenty of notice. Generally, it is 24 hours, but you will want to check to see what the requirements are in your state.

Remember that your tenants have a right to privacy, and this means they shouldn't have to worry about you showing up on the doorstep unannounced. Most states allow the landlord to enter the property for repairs and to perform inspections as long as they give notice first. They can also enter the property for emergencies such as gas leaks or water leaks, and in those cases, they do not need to provide notice.

When you are performing an inspection, you are going to be looking for different types of dangerous or unsavory conditions. If a tenant is injured on the property, the landlord is responsible for their injuries. You want to make sure that your property abides by safety and health regulations and that there are no repairs that you need to make.

You can also look for any evidence of criminal activity that could be taking place on the premises. While this is rare, it can and does happen on occasion. There could also be criminal activity in the surrounding area that has nothing to do with your tenants. In order to improve the safety of your tenants, you may want to check the security features again during the inspection and add anything that might be missing, such as security lighting or upgraded locks on the windows.

Prompt Repairs

Landlords also need to make sure that they take care of repairs as soon as possible. In some cases, the repairs will be relatively simple and you can probably do them on your own. For example, something simple such as painting the fence, replacing a missing tile, and the like are easy enough to do.

Once the tenants let you know about the problem, or when you notice it during an inspection, you can set up a time to fix it. If it isn't something that you are able to handle on your own, then you will want to get in touch with one of the contractors that you *should* have already found.

When you complete all of your repairs promptly, it will ensure that your tenants are happy and that their home is safe. Happy tenants usually will usually mean tenants that are going to stay at the property longer, which will cut down on vacancies.

Start With Just One

When you break down the things that you need to do when investing in your first rental property, it seems easy enough to handle, and really, *it is*. However, that doesn't mean that you should strive to become a real estate mogul all at once! You should start with just a single property, and once you have everything under control and running smoothly (including growing equity and a monthly income from the property), you can think about buying another home.

After you have a second property, it becomes even easier to grow and expand. It also means that it will start to become more difficult to handle everything on your own. That's especially true when it comes to properties that aren't in your hometown. In the following chapter, we will be covering more on working with property managers outside of the state.

CHAPTER 16:
HOW TO WORK WITH PROPERTY MANAGERS OUTSIDE OF YOUR STATE

When you are looking at properties outside of the state, you know that you will need to work with a property manager and that just *any* old property manager simply won't do. You want to work with a property manager who is able to maximize your returns and minimize your expenses. That means more money for you and fewer headaches worrying about the property.

While we talked about this briefly earlier in the book, it deserves its own chapter, just like managing property in your own town. We will discuss the things that you need to look for in a property management company so you can choose the best one for your needs.

What to Look for in the Perfect Property Management Company

The following are things that I, and most others, consider to be very important when it comes to choosing a property management company. Let's look at the things that you need to look for and learn *why* they are so important.

How Long Have They Been in Business and What's Their Reputation?

Is a company that has been in business for fifteen years automatically the best property management company for you to choose? No, but if they have been in business for a long time, it generally means that they are doing things right. You should try to find a company that has been in business for at least five years. This ensures that they have been around long enough to know what they are doing when it comes to property management, at least most of the time.

You can't take a long time in business at face value, though. You also need to consider their reputation. Of course, they will tell you that they have a great reputation and that the clients and tenants all love working with them. They are trying to get your business, after all!

You are going to need to dig a little bit deeper though so you can be sure you are actually working with a company that's worth your time. One of the best things to do is start looking at the review sites. You can find reviews of these companies on a number of different sites online.

If you find a number of tenants complaining about the same behaviors and issues regarding the company, then it could be that the property management company has some serious issues. Keep in mind that there will always be some tenants that will leave bad reviews because they had to pay late fees or because they were evicted. When you read the reviews, you need to be able to separate the legitimate complaints from the complaints by people who simply didn't abide by their tenant agreement.

In addition to looking at reviews from tenants who have dealt with the company, you should try to find some reviews from other investors who are working with the company or who have worked with them in the past.

Do They Have Their Own Rentals?

Here's another important one. Do the property managers have their own rental properties that they manage? If they do, it could be a good thing or a bad thing, and you will have to decide how you feel about it.

Here's what I mean. If they have their own rental properties, you might look at this as welcome news since it means they know everything that needs to happen with the property. The have experience and they can bring that experience to your rental property.

However, you also have to think about the flipside. If they have a large number of their own properties, it could mean that you and your tenants are in competition against the property management company's other properties and tenants. They might be giving their own tenants more attention and better treatment. If your property is vacant and in need of some new tenants and they have a unit that needs new tenants as well, there is always a chance that they could favor their property and show it to new tenants before they show yours.

The reviews that you read, and the information you glean from other investors who have used the company should give you a good idea of how they do business and whether you need to worry if they have their own rental units or not. In some cases, it can be a good thing. Other times, you need to beware.

Do They Know How to Screen Tenants?

You know all of the work that you went through to screen tenants before you decided to rent to them? It is vital that you make sure the property management company you are using does the same thing. You would think it is standard, but there are some unscrupulous companies out there that will cut corners and try to cut costs when it comes to background checks. They are only interested in getting bodies into the property, and they do not perform proper background checks.

I don't have to tell you what a nightmare this could become. You could have illegal activity going on at the property, you could have renters who don't pay rent on time or at all, and you could have to go through an eviction process. With proper screening, you could eliminate 98% of problem tenants before renting to them.

Ask the company about the process they use to screen tenants and see how thorough it is. You could also request that you be provided the reports and information on the tenants so that you will have the final say on who gets the property. If they aren't willing to provide you with reports, it could very well be because they simply aren't running them! Some states will not allow the property management company to provide the report because of the privacy act. But you want them to tell you in writing about monthly debts, credit score, eviction, rental history, and collections on their credit and criminal records. You need to look at the report, but you want truthful information about the tenants so you can be informed about the entire process.

The tenant-screeing process is the most critical step, so do not to take it lightly. You will save expenses in the long run. Once you go through the detailed screening process, you will select the right tenants for your property: tenants less likely to be delinquent on their rent, take better care of your property, and who will not cost you money with evictions. They will turn in the move-out notice and also cooperate with having the property available for showing.

Look for Their Name on the BBB

This is something that you should always do no matter who you are hiring. Check out the Better Business Bureau to see the property management company's rating. It's simple enough to do. Go to BBB.org and then type in the name of the business, along with their location, in the page's search bar. This will bring up the company and you can see whether they are accredited by the BBB or not, and you can see if there are any complaints about the company. You can also see their grade.

The BBB provides grades for businesses from A+ to F. Just like in school, companies that have low grades aren't doing so well, and you will want to avoid them at all costs. However, you *can't use this as your sole research*. Sometimes, people don't report companies to the BBB (even though they should), and this can cause a company to have a higher grade than they deserve.

What you want to do is use this search in addition to all of the other research that you do on the company.

How Large Is the Office and How Many on Staff?

Many new real estate rental investors feel that bigger is better, and I'm here to tell you that is not the case. Just because a company is large does not mean they do a good job. In fact, with large companies, things (including tenants) can get lost in the shuffle.

Ideally, you want to work with a smaller company that has about ten people on staff and that manages a *maximum* of 250 properties. Any more than this with a staff of this size is too much and the properties and tenants will not get the attention that they deserve.

In addition, make sure you ask how many properties are managed by each staff member. You don't want your property to be managed by someone who is overworked. If they have more than twenty-five properties, it's too much.

Even More Things to Think About With Property Management Companies

Above, we talked about some of the most important things to consider when you are looking for a property management company. However, I believe there are still some other things that you will want to know about the company before you hire them.

One of the things that you will want to talk about with the company is how often they actually get into the property. There are a number of companies out there that have a "rent it and forget it" philosophy, and that's the last thing that you want. They should be inspecting the property every six months, just as you will be doing for the properties that are in your hometown.

They should not charge extra for this service. It should be a standard part of their process. It helps to ensure the safety of the property and safety for the tenants. If a company tries to charge for this, you might want to ask how much they charge to have the inspection done. If it is $100/year, then it is worth the cost to have the property inspection twice a year.

When you are interviewing the property manager and discussing what they will do for you, pay attention to the way they communicate with you, as well as other people in the company. Are they rude? Do they constantly cut you off when you are trying to talk and ask questions? Are they actually providing answers to the questions you ask or are they talking around the questions instead? If they are treating you like this already, imagine how much worse it will be once you start to work with them.

You should expect the company to take care of maintenance and repair issues as well. Most will do this. However, you need to know how their system works. You want to make sure that you get the maintenance and repairs completed as quickly as possible, so you can give the property management company permission to take a portion of your cash flow to take care of the issues. However, you need to set a *maximum* amount that they can use before they need to obtain your permission. You should set this between $200 and $250 at most. You should require that they obtain your written permission first if the repair is over $250.

Of course, you also need to know how much all of this is going to cost you. Most of the time, a property management company is going to charge around 7% to 10% of the rent for their services. Therefore, if a company is charging 10% and the rent of the property is $1500 a month, they will receive $150 for their service each month. As you can see, this will eat away at a portion of your cash flow, but if you are out of state, you don't really have any other choice. Always know what they are charging and what services your money is buying.

Finally, let's talk about getting paid. The property manager needs to commit to paying you and providing reports on the same day of the month each month. Generally, you will want them to pay you by the 6th of the month. If you don't get them on that date, it's time to call the property manager and find out why. It could be a case of slow mail or lost mail – those things do happen. However, if it continues to happen, it is time to start looking for another property management company. I had a company that took two months' rent income from a dozen of properties they manage for us and they close their office and we could never get that money back. We did file a compliant with BBB.

In the next chapter, we will talk about what you need to do in case you discover the property management company you hired simply isn't working out for you.

CHAPTER 17:
UNEXPECTED EVENTS

No matter how much you prepare and no matter how much time and effort you spend to make sure everything goes perfect with all of your rentals, strange things can and will happen. You need to have a good idea of what these different events could be and how to solve those problems. That's exactly what we will be covering in this chapter. When you have contingencies in place for things such as this, you will find that you can weather just about anything that comes your way.

- Vacancy rate
- Maintenance
- Tenant turnover
- Tenant eviction
- Property management is not performing

Vacancy Rate

In the world of landlords, vacancy is a dirty word. Nobody likes to hear it and nobody even likes to think about it. When you have rental properties that are vacant, it means you aren't making money on them. In fact, it means you are losing money, since you still have to pay for the mortgage each month, as well as maintenance and potential repairs, taxes, insurance, and more.

It's scary, but there are some things that you can do to make it a little easier on yourself.

First, you can reduce the chance of this happening in the first place by adhering to the advice in this book. Do your research first and only invest in areas that meet the prerequisites – growing population and industries, good neighborhood, etc. Know what the average vacancy rate is like in the area before you invest. You don't want to invest in an area that has a high vacancy rate!

Of course, things still happen. There will still come times when you have a vacant property that is in desperate need of a tenant. What are you going to do to ensure you get one?

You need to act right away. As soon as you know that a tenant is moving out or that they are being evicted, you need to start marketing. Use the same marketing tips that we covered earlier in the book. The same day that the tenants leave is when you or your repair professionals need to start work to get the property ready for the next tenants. As long as there is not any major damage, this should be relatively easy.

You also need to make sure that you are pricing the property correctly. You can't "guess" at the right price, and you can't always use the price that you had for the previous tenants. You need to reassess the area's average rent for comparable properties. If you price your property too high, it is going to be difficult to find tenants that will bite. They will simply move on to one of the cheaper properties as long as it is similar. Of course, you can't price too low, either. You still need to have positive cash flow after you have paid for all of the expenses. Find the sweet spot.

Something else that you might want to consider is increasing the length of your lease. Instead of having a six-month lease, or even a year-long lease, you could offer a two-year lease to tenants. This is a big commitment from the tenant, and you might need to "sweeten" the deal a bit by offering an incentive. For example, you might want to offer to pay for one of their utilities, or for cable, for the length of the lease.

This is sure to get people's attention, and it is going to cost you far less than having a property that stands vacant for several months.

You might also find that it is easier to have a property management company, as they are able to take care of the marketing and help to fill the vacancies.

By taking the time to find quality tenants in the first place, and by providing the clients with quality service while they are living at the property, you will find that they tend to stick around a lot longer. This means lower vacancy rates for you.

Maintenance

You strive to take great care of the property, but sometimes things go wrong. A windstorm could tear away part of the roof or blow a branch through a window. There could be a plumbing problem. There could be any number of things that require maintenance, and they always seem like a nightmare to the unprepared landlord.

The key to dealing with this problem is to be prepared. You want to make it as easy as possible for your tenants to reach you in the event they need maintenance or a repair on the property. Once they get in touch, you need to check out the problem and talk with the correct professional about taking care of the problem.

I mentioned it before, but it definitely bears repeating here. You need to have a list of professionals that you can contact for repairs, *before* you actually have any maintenance or repairs to make. As soon as you choose a property, you need to start looking at the best contractors and handymen in the area that you can call on when needed. Research these professionals just as you would a property management company.

In addition, you can reduce the cost of repairs by making sure that you are conducting walkthroughs of the property every few months, as we talked about. This will let you know if there are any maintenance issues that the tenants haven't informed you of, and it's cheaper to deal with them sooner rather than later once they get worse.

You should also be setting aside some money each month to put into a maintenance fund for the property. This way, if there are repairs, you will be able to dip into that fund rather than paying out of your own pocket. Remember, you have to run this like a business--because it is a business!

Tenant Turnover

Tenant turnover, whether they move out or are evicted, can be a real killer to your cash flow. You have to think about all of the costs associated with moving a tenant out of the home, getting it ready, and moving another tenant into the place. There are administrative costs to process the tenants in and out, as well as your marketing costs. You have to consider the time and money of showing the property, the cost of running background checks, cost of repair, and the amount of income you are losing. This ties in closely with vacancy rates, and if you aren't careful, you will have a vacant property.

Just as with vacancy rates, you can do some simple things that will help to keep your units occupied so you can avoid tenant turnover. You'll see that these are quite similar to dealing with vacancies.

Always respond to the tenant requests, whether they need a repair or they are having issues with other neighbors. Be responsive and communicate openly with them. Also, make sure you are maintaining your properties, as this will make the turnover process much faster.

Something else that you should do when you are looking for tenants is to look at the length of time they generally spend in a unit. If they move every year, it means that they will probably stay at your property for only a single year. This means that you will be looking forward to another turnover at the end of the lease. Try to avoid these types of tenants if at all possible.

Doing these things and keeping your rent reasonable for the area are the best ways to reduce tenant turnover. In the event that you do have tenants that leave, just make sure that you get the property back onto the market as quickly as possible so you aren't without the rental income.

Do not increase rent payments at the market rate. Keep it at a minimum 5% below market rate so that tenant will stay longer. You can cut thousands in turnover tenant expenses by keeping the rent below market rate.

Tenant Eviction

No one likes the idea of an eviction. You hate the thought of putting someone out of a home, but you hate the idea that they aren't paying rent or that they are causing damage to the property even more. You might be a great landlord, but that does not mean that you will always have good tenants.

The goal is to have as few bad tenants as possible. Proper screening is going to help you reduce the number of undesirable renters, but there is still a chance that you could end up with a tenant that is nothing but trouble. You want to be nice, but you also need to be strict when it comes to the policies you have in place, including paying the rent on time.

Although eviction seems harsh, sometimes it is necessary, and you need to know what you have to do in case it comes to that.

First, you should look up the eviction laws in the states where you have property, as they differ across the country. When you are creating your lease agreement, you should have these laws in mind so that you and the tenants understand what will happen in the event of an eviction.

Second, you need to contact an attorney. If you did as was suggested earlier in the book, you will have an attorney that you can call when you need to have help with an eviction. Keep in mind that you can't perform an eviction on your own. It is illegal to do any of the following on your own; .

- Remove the tenant's belongings from the house or the property
- Remove the tenant physically
- Change the locks
- Shut off utilities that are essential
- Harass the tenant

You need to have a valid reason for evicting the tenants from the property. As long as you have given fair notice to the tenant, there are a number of things that will be considered reason for eviction by the courts. If the tenant fails to pay their rent, violates the lease agreement, damages the property, causes health and safety hazards, or breaks occupancy or noise ordinances, it is possible to evict them.

In order to do so, you need to have documentation that proves your claims against the tenant. If you find that the only course of action is to evict the tenant, then you need to follow through. You need to provide them with the notice of eviction, which your attorney can prepare for you. The attorney will make sure that you supply the tenants with the proper notice.

Once you provide the notice, and they don't change their ways or pay their rent, you can file the eviction case with the court. You will need to bring your proof to the court hearing. These can include things such as the lease agreement, payment records, bounced checks, communication records, a copy of the notice you provided to the renters, and proof that they received the notice.

If you win the case, the tenant will then be provided with a certain amount of time before they need to vacate the premises. In the event that they are not out of the unit within that timeframe, you can have someone from the county sheriff's department escort them and their belongings out of the property.

Avoiding Eviction

It might be possible to avoid eviction in some cases. You can talk with the tenants about the issues that they are causing. Sometimes, simply talking with them can straighten out the problem and you can avoid having them leave altogether. This is the ideal situation, as it means you will not have to worry about having a vacant home that you need to rent.

Other times, they will leave on their own because they do not want to deal with an eviction any more than you do. Instead of meeting at the rental house or your home, it's a good idea to have this conversation with the tenant in a public location. They are more likely to stay calm when they are in public.

When you explain what eviction can do to them, you will find that they are usually more than willing to leave. Eviction will damage their credit score, which will make it impossible for them to get a loan or even a credit card for quite a while. In addition, you can sue them for back rent, and you can garnish their wages for the money. When you show them how much simpler everything will be if they just leave on their own, most see the wisdom in it, and you can avoid the eviction process.

Collecting Back Rent

What happens if the renter still owes a substantial amount of back rent? You do not want to let this go, and fortunately, you have several courses of action that you could take. You might want to take the case to small claims court, which could result in the tenant's wages being garnished. The court could also garnish their tax refund. You could also choose to use a private debt collector to take care of the money that's owed to you.

The ultimate goal is to avoid this situation entirely with proper screening. If you have had several bad tenants, then there could be something wrong with the screening that you or your property management company is using. It's time to take another look at how you are vetting the tenants so you can reduce the chance of this happening again in the future.

Property Management Is Not Performing

When you have a lot of local properties or your properties are out of state, having a property management company can be a lifesaver. We've already covered how to find a good company, but sometimes things just don't work out. Sometimes, you may find that the property management company is not performing the way you need them to or they may have breached the contract, so you need to end the relationship. Here's how do you do it.

First, you need to look at the management contract that you signed with the company and find the termination clause. Most contracts will have a 30- to 90-day termination clause. You need to let the company know in writing that you are requesting termination of your contract and provide them with plenty of notice.

When you send in your request, make sure that you send it by certified mail with a return receipt request. This way, you know that it arrived at the property manager. Make sure that the notice has the effective date of termination. In some cases, the clause will require that you provide a reason. If so, then you need to provide the reason in your notification. If you try to terminate the contract without reason, it could be considered a breach of contract, which could lead to legal trouble.

In addition, you need to check to see whether there are any termination fees. The fees can vary. They could be just a few hundred dollars. However, they might also be enough to cover the management fees for the remainder of the contract.

You should also let your tenants know that there will be a change of management. In some cases, the contract might specify that the property management company will take care of this, but you will still want to touch base with the tenants and let them know. Provide them with information regarding who will be taking care of their needs going forward, and who is holding their deposit money.

It is also important that you never make your relationships with the property management company, or any of your contractors, personal.

This is because it can cloud your judgment and you might end up giving them too much leeway when they don't take care of maintenance or when they do not pay you on time. It is a business relationship, and you need to sever your relationship so you can find a company that will produce the results you need for your investment.

Refer to Chapter 15 so you can refresh your memory on what it takes to find a good property management company that has the best interests of you and your property in mind. Without a good property management company, your investment is going to suffer.

PART 5:

Exit Strategy

CHAPTER 18:
SELLING YOUR RENTAL

As you know by now, I feel that buying and holding onto property for your rentals is the best solution when it comes to growing wealth. *Most* of the time, you will want to make sure that you hold on to those properties forever, as it means you will always have a source of passive income.

However, there are certain things that might get you to the point when you need to sell one of the rental properties. Here are some of the reasons that you may find that selling your property makes the most financial sense.

- Economic change
- People are moving out of the area
- Negative cash flow

Economic Change

When you see the winds of economic change blowing through, it might be time to contemplate selling. If there are a number of businesses that are leaving the area, or just one of the major employers, it could mean bad news for the neighborhood. It might mean that it will be more difficult to find renters in the future, which ties in with the next reason to sell.

People Are Moving Out of the Area

If people are moving out of the area, then it means the pool of renters is going to be much smaller. This means that refilling vacancies will take longer and that you will be losing money on your investment. When you notice that there is a shift in the number of people in the neighborhood, as well as economic changes, you should think about selling as well.

Negative Cash Flow

This one should be very evident. If you notice that you can't keep a positive cash flow in the property, then it is certainly time to sell. Maybe the rents in the area have gone down and people aren't willing to pay the rent that you set. If you are going negative each month, you are losing money, and that's the worst situation for a rental property owner.

Now that you know some of the reasons that selling would be in your best interest, it's time to learn how to sell properly.

Selling Your Rental Property

Selling a piece of investment property is quite different from selling other types of investments. You can't simply make a phone call or click a couple of buttons as you would if you had to sell stocks, for example. It can take weeks or months to sell a piece of property, and you have to think about the taxes that are involved with the sale. If you are selling so you can buy another property in another area, you may be able to avoid the capital gains tax (Internal Revenue Code Section 1031). Otherwise, you will have to pay taxes on the sale of the property.

If you do qualify for a 1031 exchange, you will have a time limit of 45 days to choose another property to buy and six months to complete the transaction. If this is your goal, it is a good idea to start looking for a new rental property before you sell the current one.

Talk with a real estate and tax professional to get a better understanding of your situation, so you can be sure you are making the right decision for your finances.

Once you decide what you want to do – simply sell or roll over with the 1031 – you will go about selling the property just as you would any home. Make sure the place is in good shape, let the current renters know that you are selling and ask them if they are interested in buying, and speak with a real estate agent.

Now, you will be on the opposite end of negotiations when you are trying to sell. You want to get as much as possible for the property. If the neighborhood is suffering from economic trouble, you might not be able to find another investor who is interested in the property. However, there are still likely some people who are looking for their personal home and who might be interested, especially if you have managed to keep the property in good shape.

What Is the 1031 Exchange?

The 1031 exchange is something that can become very important for real estate rental investors such as yourself. Also called a Starker or a like-kind exchange, it is a literal exchange of one investment asset for another. If you qualify, this can help you reduce or eliminate taxes when you make the exchange. This is true even if you have a profit during the swap of properties.

Essentially, you are selling one property and using that money to invest in another property. It is important to have help from a professional tax advisor to understand whether you qualify and how to go about it correctly. I also wanted to share with you some "need to know" information about the 1031 exchange so you can get a better idea of what it is in regard to real estate.

You Can't Use It for Personal Property

You can use the 1031 exchange only when you are exchanging one investment property for another. You can't do it for personal property in most situations, and since you are going to be doing this only for your rental properties, you don't have to worry about anything such as vacation properties.

You Need to Designate the Replacement Property

You need to think about the timing when you are exchanging your property. You need to designate a replacement property within 45 days of the sale of the first property in writing, while a third party holds the cash (you can't receive cash for the exchange). You are able to designate up to three properties at this time, as long as you close on one of them. There are some cases where you could designate more than three, but only when the fair market value of the properties don't go over 200% of the fair market value of the exchanged properties. Your real estate and tax advisor can help you with this process.

Close in Six Months

You also need to make sure that you are closing within six months of the sale of the old property. As soon as the old property closes, this time starts counting down. It is always a good idea to have some properties in mind even before you sell and try to get the 1031 exchange so you do not miss the window.

Cash Received Is Taxed

If there is cash left over after the purchase of the new property, you will receive it at the end of the six months. However, this cash that you receive *will* be taxed as capital gain. You just won't have to pay taxes on the entire sale thanks to the exchange.

Try to Hold

As I've said, the ideal situation is to be able to hold on to the property forever. It can represent a passive income for you for the rest of your life, and in most cases, there is no reason to get rid of it. If managing the properties on your own is getting to be too much trouble, work with a property management company. You will still have a substantial amount of income, but you will have fewer day-to-day things to worry about with the business.

PART 6:

Building Your Financial Future

CHAPTER 19:
CAN YOU BUY A RENTAL WHEN YOU HAVE A FULL-TIME JOB?

So, at this point in the book, you are probably starting to get the itch to look into potential investments in your area. That's great. However, there are likely quite a few of you who are still a bit skeptical about getting into the field since you have a full-time job right now. You don't know if you can devote enough time and energy to running a rental property.

By now, you should see that running a rental property that you own really isn't that difficult. You just need to make sure you do the research and get all of the pieces in place when you buy. In fact, there are quite a few people out there who are keeping their full-time jobs for now and investing in real estate rentals.

It's a great solution for many different types of people as well. Let's look at some examples of the different sorts of folks out there that can benefit from keeping their full-time job and working with rentals.

A doctor or an attorney typically has a high income. They can use the tax deductions that come with property ownership to help them keep their taxes under control. People who are working in other professional areas will find that they like the fact that they can work at the job they actually love while building wealth with real estate.

Perhaps you are a stay-at-home mom or dad that wants to help with the family finances. Even though you have a lot to do when you are taking care of the kids and everything else at the house, you can get into real estate rentals to start bringing in some extra money. Young adults could also start investing in rental properties while they are working full-time as a way to help build up their retirement funds.

What do all of these people have in common? Even though they might have different jobs and be in different stages of their life right now, they are all looking forward to the future and they are planning for it. They are putting the pieces in place to have a continual passive income so they can grow their wealth with rental properties. I believe you can do the same.

You do need to figure out how to strike the perfect balance between both of these aspects of your life though. Lucky for you, that's what we'll be covering in the next section.

What I've found is that it is actually *better* for people to continue with their full-time job when they are starting out with rental investments. One of the big benefits is that you will be able to save more money for the down payment. Remember, the larger your down payment, the lower the mortgage is going to be, since you have less to pay. You could use the additional money to pay down the mortgage (and build equity) faster, or you could have the money as extra income.

Until you have enough rental income, you can keep your full-time job. When you find that your rental income is high enough, you can decide to go into the rental business full-time if you choose. It's very achievable. You can work for ten years and then invest in one house at a time (one a year is good), continually adding to your properties until you have plenty of cash flow to support the lifestyle that you want. The longer you do this, and the more homes you buy, the greater your wealth will be.

Some people might be in a different situation. A number of people I know have the money to put down on ten different houses at once, which is able to generate enough of an income for them that they can quit their current job right away. They can just focus on their real estate rental business and take it to the next level.

Basically, I am saying that there is more than one path to success with this type of investing.

You can keep your full-time job for the rest of your life and do rentals on the side. You could keep your job just until you are making enough money to generate the income needed to satisfy the lifestyle that you want. You could also buy ten properties right now if you have the cash. You might even get to the point where you can go part-time with your regular work and put more time into the rental business, while still making the same amount of money as when you were working full-time.

The beauty of this method is that it is something that you can do in a manner that *suits you*. Find the path that works and get started.

How Do You Balance Your Job and Your Real Estate Business?

Right now, you might be thinking that it would be impossible to balance your current work schedule with a rental real estate business. You also have friends, family, and hobbies that you like to partake in sometimes. It might seem difficult to get to the point where you can handle both of these jobs. I'm here to say that it's *entirely possible*. You simply need to be focused and organized. So, how do you that?

Focus and Dedication

If you go into any activity in life, no matter what it is, with a negative or defeatist attitude, you are not going to succeed. You need to develop a positive attitude and believe that you will succeed.

In addition, you need to be dedicated to achieving your goals. In the next chapter, we will be discussing quite a bit about those goals and what you need to do to reach them. You also need to be dedicated to constant learning. This book is a good start, but there will always be new things to learn, and you should absorb as much as possible. The more you know, the better your decisions will be.

Know your goals and dedicate yourself to take action achieving them. You must be persistent, even when things look like they might not be going your way. When you come up against obstacles, do not let them stop you. Find ways over, under, or around them.

Even though you are focused and dedicated to your rental business, that doesn't mean that you can't give 100% at work. You still need to put in the time and effort needed for your 9 to 5 as you would even if you weren't running your rental business.

Getting Organized

I've found that you can't do much of anything unless you are organized and have a plan. Your rental business is a *business*, as I've said quite a few times. Create a business plan and then start to develop your own system for each step that we've discussed. Develop a system for researching.

Here's something to you need to know about creating systems and workflows. Your first attempt might not be perfect. In fact, it probably won't be. You need to refine them as you proceed to make sure they work for you. As you progress and become more adept at each of the different elements, from research to marketing and collecting rent from tenants, you will find the system that works best for you.

Once you have a good system in place, you will find that every subsequent property you buy becomes much easier simply by following the system that you have in place. It really does become easier as you go. When you are organized, you do not have to worry about finding the phone numbers and paperwork that you need. Everything will be in place and ready to go, and that will end up giving your more time to work on other projects.

Start Slowly

Building your wealth with real estate rentals is not a sprint. It's a marathon. You will be building your properties slowly. When you are first starting, you can and should take your time. Put in plenty of research, create your business plan, and then start looking for your first invest-ment in the back yard. Take things just one step at a time and you will get there. Doing it this way also ensures you aren't burning the candle at both ends, so you can keep your full-time job and still work on growing your rental business.

Change Some Elements of Your Lifestyle

Don't worry; I'm not going to suggest that you spend less time with your family and friends, or that you give up on all of your hobbies. I'm not going to suggest that you stop going to the gym or having fun either. What I do suggest you do is look at your current web habits and television viewing habits.

If we're being honest with ourselves, there is probably a substantial amount of time each day that you are wasting on things that will not further your career and grow your wealth. A little bit of downtime on the web and with your favorite television shows is certainly fine. It's good to relax.

However, if you are spending several hours a night binging shows on Netflix and Hulu, or you spend an inordinate amount of time admir-ing cat videos on the web, then it might be time to cut back on those things. Most people come home, spend a little time with their family, and plop down in front of the television or their tablet or computer. Watch only the shows that are really important to you, and cut down on the amount of time that you spend surfing the web aimlessly.

How much time are *you* spending doing this? Let's say that you are only spending two hours a day wasting time on the web or watching television shows and movies (many people spend five to six hours a day doing this!). Now, cut out that wasted time. If you are able to save just two hours a day, that's ten hours a week and forty hours in a month. That's like getting an *extra week* of time in the month that you could be spending working on your rental business--and you won't even miss it.

You can save all of those television shows and cat videos to watch once you have passive income and more time to waste!

How Can You Invest Out of State With a Full-Time Job?

Earlier in the book, I mentioned that you need to make sure that you need to spend at least two weeks in an area while you are researching it and building your out-of-state team. If you have a full-time job, how is this possible? It can be difficult, depending on the type of job you have. However, if you have a company that offers vacation time, I suggest saving up two weeks of vacation so you can visit the location.

Remember, you should not start investing in real estate rentals outside of your area or your state for a few years. You want to have several properties already under your belt, which are bringing in money each month. At that point, you could request an unpaid two-week leave from your job. Some workplaces will be accommodating, while others will not be.

Another option is to find someone that you trust and that you have helped to understand the real estate rental business go in your stead. After you do the research at home, they can head to the neighborhood and finish the research, and they can report back to you. They could even provide you with photos and videos so you have a better sense of being there.

While this is not exactly the same as being there on your own, sometimes, it's the only option, and it is the next-best thing. Just make sure that the person who is reporting back to you understands the types of things they should be looking for in the neighborhoods and the properties.

This doesn't mean that you should never visit the area, though. Once the initial research is done and you have located some potential properties, you might want to take a weekend business trip to look at those units. It's not the same as getting two weeks to experience the area, but it will let you know more about the actual properties that interest you so you can see if it is a good idea or if you want to pass.

Just make sure that you speak with the real estate agents who are showing the property ahead of time so they can accommodate you when you arrive and need to see the property. It's not going to be a glamorous, fun-filled vacation, but it's not about that. It's about business.

It will be a tight schedule to get in and out in the matter of a weekend, and it might seem like a waste of money for the flight. Don't look at it like that, though. Instead, look at this as part of the investment. It's far better to spend a few hundred dollars to determine whether the property is worth your time or not than it is to spend a few hundred thousand dollars on a bad piece of property.

Once you know it is the right city to invest more, then hire a local project manager to do all the tasks for you each time you acquire a new property. I do it in some states because I have a trusted local project manager to run the whole team from acquire/fix the property ready for rent and then turn it over to the property manager to manage and market it for rent.

Transitioning to Full-Time Investing

Different investors will reach this point at different times in their career. Some might be ready after just two or three years, while others might be ready after a decade of keeping their full-time job. However, you need to look before you leap. Make sure that your finances are in shape and that you will be able to make enough money to live comfortably without having a full-time or part-time job.

As I said earlier, you don't have to move too quickly. Every investor is different. Move as fast as you are comfortable. In fact, there are some investors in rental real estate who remain at their full-time job until they retire because they like it.

In the next chapter, we will be talking about your financial goals and how you will be going about creating financial independence.

CHAPTER 20:
YOUR FINANCIAL GOALS

I am not your financial advisor so it is your responsibility to seek for professional financial adviser's help to deepen your objective to achieve financial independence. Below are some of my personal experiences that have worked for me.

It is very important that you understand your financial goals for the near future, as well as for your retirement and beyond. In this chapter, we will be looking at how you can achieve those financial goals and to give you some tips on helping to make it a bit easier so you can start really investing in rental real estate.

What Are Your Financial Goals Right Now?

The first thing that you need to do is determine *where* you are right now.

What are your finances like?

How much money do you make and how much are you spending each month?

Are you in debt, and if so, by how much?

Knowing where you are and where you want to be over the course of the next couple of years is a good place to start. Once you figure this out, it will be easier for you to set a course for the rest of your life when it comes to your wealth and finances.

Once you start to take control of your finances, you will see that you are able to meet your goals. It does take some time and discipline, though.

I came to this country in my early twenties and I did not have any-thing except a few pieces of clothing in my suitcase, but through hard work and commitment, I took consistent actions to reach my financial goals, which include health, family, happiness, and charity contribution. It was not as easy as it looks; I had no family members to support me for college tuition so I had to work at McDonalds, at a nursing home, at a printing company, as a babysitter, and at the com-puter lab at school, just because I did not want to have full load of debt after I graduated. I graduated with no student debt. I then landed a corporate job after finishing my double college degrees. After all the hard work, suddenly I felt that my life and finances were being controlled by a lot of third parties. I decided to take my financial future into my own hands after my last company shut down because it ran out of funding. *Life is full of events, and you become wiser and gain clarity of what you really want out of life after you experience so much, like I did.*

I took the courage to change to a career to finance, and specialized in residential mortgages. I opened my mortgage company after exten-sive training though a mortgage expert who had been working in the mortgage business for over 35 years. 2001 was the year that I started both the mortgage company and the real estate investment business. I have achieved financial independence though real estate investments in 2008. I am very grateful that I got my time back to focus on things that truly matter to me and give meaning to my life.

During these eight years, I did have a very clear plan of what to do each year to achieve my goals, and having a plan kept me focused and on course. Yes, both businesses had up and down like any busi-ness, but having a plan helped me to know what I needed to learn and the areas that I could improve to take my business to the next level.

It's always good to have a plan and implement it consistently daily until you reach your goals.

Your Debt

The vast majority of people out there have at least some debt. The goal is to pay off this debt so you do not need to worry about being behind on bills, and so you can keep building a good credit score. When you are out of debt, you will have full control over your income, and that is going to leave you with more money to put into investments. Being out of debt will also make it easier for you to quit your full-time job sooner if you want to focus solely on real estate rentals.

Of course, the biggest benefit of clearing away all of your debt is the fact that your mind will be at ease. You will not have to worry about bills piling up. Life without this stress feels amazing, and it is a goal that is definitely worth working toward.

To remove your debt, you can refer to the chapter on building good credit for some tips. Essentially, you want to make sure that you don't carry debt on your credit cards and that you pay off your loans. This can take some serious rearranging of your lifestyle for a while, as you will see later in the chapter. However, I firmly believe that it is well worth some temporary sacrifices.

Learn to Live on Less Than You Make

One of the most important things that I hope you take away from this chapter is this: Be able to live on less than you are bringing home. It's a simple thing, really, but it might surprise you how many people have trouble with this. They always want the biggest, best, and newest *thing*. They are chasing these things rather than chasing wealth – which would eventually allow them to get all of the things they want, funnily enough.

What do I mean by living on less than you make? Simply this. You need to be able to pay for all of your bills and still have money left over that you can use for removing debt (as mentioned), and to use for savings and investments. If you find that you can't do this, then it is time to look at your lifestyle to see what the problem might be.

Before you buy any big items what will reduce in value, then you should think three times—for example, a new car. Should you put it off until you can buy a property that generates enough income to cover your car payment? That way, you can always drive the car you want, and your rental will pay for it.

Build an Emergency Fund

Just as you need to have an emergency fund set aside for repairs on your property, you need to have a fund set up for your life. It is one of the first financial goals that you should strive to achieve, as it can help to give you a cushion and more peace of mind, just in case something happens. Your goals should be to have enough money in the fund to cover several months (a minimum of six months of expenses) just in case.

We will talk more about saving for emergency funds and other needs in the next section.

How Much Can You Save from Your Current Job After Expenses?

Everyone is likely to have a different answer here, as it will depend on how much you make and how many expenses you need to pay each month. When you are trying to make a plan to reach your financial goals, though, it becomes something that is extremely important for you to answer. It should be very simple to calculate.

Consider how much money you bring in from your job after taxes. If you are married or have a partner and you are going to be going into this business together, you will want to take his or her income into account as well.

Once you have the sum of your income after your taxes, you need to write down all of your essential bills each month. How much are you paying for your own mortgage or rent? How much are you paying for your car payments, insurance, food, and all of the other things that you need or want throughout the month? The number that you have left over is the amount that you are able to save after you have paid all of your expenses.

Go ahead and calculate that right now if you haven't already. Are you surprised by the amount of money after expenses? Is it higher or lower than you thought it would be? This is an essential first step in developing a budget. You need to know how much you have coming in and going out, and you need to know how and where you can make some changes to increase that extra money. A big part of that probably has to do with your lifestyle, which we will be covering next.

What Is Your Lifestyle?

In this section, I want you to take a look at your current lifestyle. Are you spending money on things that you don't really need? Sure, we all like to be comfortable, and we all like to have a certain level of luxury in our life. However, when you are trying to get things off the ground with your rental properties, you will want to make sure that you re-evaluate where and how you are spending your money. You might be surprised at some very simple yet effective ways that you can increase the amount of money you have available for saving and investing each month.

These really are *simple*, and you can start making a difference today. We touched on some of these earlier in the book when we talked about improving your credit. Let's look at how you can do it!

Your Electricity and Heat

This one's an easy one. Make sure that you turn off lights and electronics when you leave the house. It's easy to forget a radio or a light, but that slowly raises your energy bill each month. Even saving just a small amount on your electricity can make a difference when you add up all of the other ways that you can save. For example, you can reduce your energy bill further by adjusting your thermostat. By changing it just a few degrees with the season, you will be able to save money and you won't really notice the difference in the temperature. You can turn it down even lower when you leave the house and before you go to bed.

Your Appliances

When do you run your appliances, such as the dishwasher and the washing machine? If you answer, "Whenever I need to," you are doing it wrong. Many utility companies have what they call peak and off-peak hours. You should check with your utility company to determine what they consider off-peak hours, as this will be the cheapest time to run your appliances.

Stop Eating Out So Much

Everyone likes to have a good meal out once in a while, and there is nothing wrong with that. However, it is a good idea to keep these to a minimum for special occasions and celebrations. You do not need to go out once or twice a week for dinner and drinks, or even for coffee in the morning.

In addition to this, you will want to stay away from fast food restaurants, as they can eat through your wallet (not to mention your stomach) faster than you realize. Let's look at the life of a fictitious person we will call Typical Jane, who is representative of how people, and perhaps you, spend money eating out each month.

Jane loves her morning coffee, and she stops at Starbucks on the way to work to get her caffeine to fuel her morning. Each morning, she spends $4 on coffee, and another $3 on a muffin or some other breakfast item. Then, she and her coworkers go out to lunch. Let's say that she spends an average of $8 for a cheap meal at lunch. When she comes home, sometimes she's too tired to cook, and will stop at a fast food place twice a week, spending another $16 total. Then, she and her significant other go out to dinner once a week and she spends $50.

Spending here and there might not seem like a lot, but let's look at the totals. In one week, she is spending $141 dollars simply eating out. That's $464 a month. Take a moment to let that soak in … $464 a month. Now, let's say she only spends about half that. That's *still* $232 a month that she could put elsewhere. She could pay down her debt or increase the amount of money she has for investing.

If she has a significant other, then the other person may have the same spending habits. This is a large amount of money!

How can you reduce this? It is simple, but it does take some work. First, you need to commit to going to the grocery store and cooking. If you are limited on time, consider cooking some meals ahead of time. A slow cooker can be great for this. Get items that you can bring for lunch so you do not need to go out to eat. Cut back on going out for dinner to once a month.

Here's a tip for when you go to the grocery store. Never go on an empty stomach or you will end up buying far more than you need, and it probably won't be healthy food either. Go when you are full and stock up on the necessities. You might also find it advantageous to buy certain things, such as rice or toilet paper, in bulk.

Also, when you are in the grocery store, stop to think about the products you are buying. Are you gravitating toward the name brands? Do you know what you are paying for with these brands? Nothing but the name and the logo in most cases. You will find that the generic products are just as good for the most part. You can save money on many of your toiletries, clothes, food, and more when you stop chasing the brands.

These little changes can help immensely, and you will even feel healthier since you will not be eating as much fast food. However, there are plenty of other ways that you can cut down on your expenses as well.

Limit Entertainment Expenses

There are quite a few ways to cut down on the amount you are spending on entertainment. Instead of going to the movies and spending a fortune for a couple of tickets, some popcorn, and some drinks, you could get a subscription to Netflix and Hulu for much less.

If you are like many people out there, you complain about cable. You have all of those channels and there is rarely anything to watch! It's true, so why do you continue to throw money at the cable company each month?

There are better ways, thanks to the internet. When you cancel cable, you could be saving $70 to $100 each month. If you have favorite shows, there are a number of cheaper options out there. Hulu is a good example, as it has many shows the day after they air, as mentioned. There are other similar services as well. You can also find the shows that you really love and buy digital versions of them. A full season of a show is often less than two months of cable television.

In addition, there are plenty of cheap and free things that you can do for entertainment. Find some hiking trails in your area. You can get some exercise and fresh air, and it isn't going to cost as much as going to see a play, for example.

This does not mean that you have to cancel your social life! Instead of going out, invite friends over. There are still plenty of things you can do for entertainment without spending a lot of money.

Your Bank's ATM

Here's one that gets just about everyone. Whenever you withdraw money from an ATM that is not from your bank, you have to pay a fee. It's often between $2 and $3, which might not seem like much. If you take money out of the ATM three times a week though, you could be spending $36 in fees. That's some wasted money!

Learn to Do Simple Things

Are you the type of person who will take clothes to the drycleaner and ask them to sew on a button or the type of person who needs to hire landscapers to mow a small lawn and trim the hedges? To be honest, those are luxury expenses, and you can handle the work yourself. Learn to sew a button, get out there and cut the lawn, and take care of all of the little repairs that you can do on your own. It's far better than wasting money having someone else to it for you just for convenience. You get some new skill sets that you can use for years.

Stop With the Credit Cards

Having a credit card for emergencies is a good idea. However, it should be for emergencies only. Millions of people in the country have fallen into the trap of relying on their credit cards for everything, including large purchases that they shouldn't buy. You would be much better served keeping the number of credit cards you have to a minimum and keeping the balances on them very low. Instead, when you are making purchases, you should try to rely on cash.

This means that it's more difficult for you to go into debt. You will also discover that it is easier to stop yourself from making purchases when you are using cash. The credit card can make a person not stop and think about the money they are spending because they never actually see the cash. They also don't think about the interest they will be paying. That $1000 television is going to cost you quite a bit more when you factor in all of that interest.

Cancel Some Subscriptions and Memberships

Do you have any magazine subscriptions, memberships to clubs, or any other type of monthly expenditures that you don't really need? If so, then it is time to cancel those subscriptions right now. Think about the things that you do and do not use and get rid of the ones that do not matter. Even if you are only saving what seems like a small sum each year by cutting subscriptions to two or three magazines, it adds up with all of these other ways to save.

These are some very easy and practical ways that you can start saving money right now. Over the course of a year, you could potentially save thousands more than you thought possible, and that's a great feeling.

However, you have to be the one willing to make these changes in your lifestyle. You need to be able to commit to the changes if you really want to see some results. If you aren't willing to make changes and sacrifices, then you will not be able to grow your wealth and create a passive income. If you do commit to the changes, though, you will see that the benefits start to pour in right away. For starters, you will not be as worried about money since you know how to save.

How Much Longer Are You Planning to Work?

For many people, the goal is to get to the point with your rental business that you do not have to work another job. You can just focus on real estate. However, you have to look at things realistically. By now, you should know where you stand financially and the things that you need to do to improve your finances and to get to the point where you can really invest.

So, just how much money will you need to make in order to quit your current job and work on rental real estate full-time? Part of this is going to depend on the lifestyle you want to have and maintain.

If you are comfortable with the bare minimum, you might be able to quit your job sooner. If you want to have money for traveling and to buy items that you want (not that you necessarily need), then you will need to make sure you are making more money from your rentals before you can retire from your other job.

Once you have determined how much you need to live comfortably, it will become easier for you to determine just how many properties you will need to have. Let's look at a simple example.

Let's say that you want to have just $6,000 a month of passive income from the rentals that you own. If you have 20 rentals after ten years of investing, and each of those rentals brings in $400 a month in positive cash flow. This means that you would be bringing in about $8000 a month, which is $2000 more than you need for living right now. This gives you plenty to live on, and it gives you extra money that you can use for investing in more real estate, putting into savings, or investing in other areas.

Right now, twenty rentals might seem like a lot, but it really isn't. Once you get a couple of properties, it becomes much easier to buy more, and this continues to create wealth for you.

Does this mean that you should stop working another job entirely? Not necessarily, but it does mean you don't have to work a job that you do not like. You can do plenty of other things with your time, including starting a fun business from one of your hobbies, if you like. There won't be as much pressure for you to make that business succeed right away. For example, if you love woodworking, you could parlay those skills into selling crafts and furniture and *still* be able to run your rental real estate business fulltime.

Of course, you might really love the idea of not doing anything other than relaxing and vacationing. Once you meet your financial goals of getting your rental business bringing in the right amount of money, then you could do that as well. When you have financial freedom, you really will feel free to follow your dreams.

Understand Your Goals and You Can Reach Them

Once you understand what your goals are, and you take the advice in this chapter to help you make some of the changes that you need, it will become much easier to actually reach those goals and to start investing in real estate. Create a plan, make changes in your life to reach your goals, and buy real estate. It's as simple as that, and it just takes some work and commitment.

CHAPTER 21:
HOW TO BECOME
A VERY SUCCESSFUL
REAL ESTATE INVESTOR

You do not want to become a real estate investor. You want to become a *successful* real estate investor--and trust me, there is a difference. Anyone with the money can invest in real estate, but only those who take the time to learn the business and who are serious about improving their status and increasing their wealth will do well. It's a business that you can succeed in as long as you are focused and driven.

Best of all, when you do succeed, you will find that you don't have to work nearly as hard to keep it going. You will have a wonderful passive income that can carry you through life. Let's look at some final tips and secrets that I believe you should take with you, as we get near the end of the book.

Review Your Budget Sheet on a Monthly Basis

It's very important that you look at your budget sheets each month. You need to make sure that you are budgeting properly and that you are not overspending, or underspending, on any of your properties. You should also have a budget sheet for your own home life and expenses, to be honest.

For your rentals, you want to know your rental income versus your expenses. While the expenses are typically the same from month to month, they can change. For example, if there is maintenance or repairs, it will alter the profits made that month. There are many little things that could cause changes in the income flow, so you need to track them in your budget sheets.

Become a Lifelong Learner

Just because you've read this book, it doesn't mean that you are done learning about real estate. You are just getting started. In fact, even those who have been in the business for years, such as myself, continue to learn every single day. There is always something new to consider. Perhaps it is a change in the regulations, or a new tool that can make budgeting easier. Maybe someone has found a better way of marketing a property.

You always want to continue to learn and add to your knowledge database. It will help you immensely in this field. I encourage learning other things as well, outside of the real estate field. There is a world of knowledge out there, and it is time that you soaked up as much as possible. I always have many interests, including better family life, health, traveling, and creating more wealth--so besides spending time with my kids, and overseeing the real estate business, I love learning more about other interests above by reading a lot of books and also attending masterminds/experts group meetings.

Set Realistic Goals and Take Massive Actions to Reach Them

You have big financial goals, naturally. However, you also want them to be realistic. Everyone will have slightly different financial goals that they want to meet, and different ways of getting to that point. The goal is to make them achievable so you do not get discouraged. You aren't going to become a millionaire in the span of a year.

However, by setting different financial milestones at three years, five years, and ten years, you can see how close you are getting to meeting your dreams, and you can make changes to the way you are conducting your business to reach those goals in the given timeframes.

You have to be willing to work hard to meet your goals, and sometimes that means taking some big actions to do it. It might mean moving beyond your state to invest in some properties, for example.

Help Others Reach Their Dreams

When you get into this field and you start to make your dreams come true, do not be surprised when you have other people who want to know the secret. There will be other investors out there who are just starting out and they want to know how you achieved your goals.

I believe that you should share your knowledge and help others to climb the ladder. There is plenty of room for everyone. In fact, that's why I wrote this book. I want to help you and others like you achieve their dreams. One of the great things about this is the fact that when you help others, it actually motivates *you* to do better and to move on to an even higher level of success.

I am very grateful for this knowledge I was able to help some of my family members and close friends to start in this business and all of them have add hundreds of thousands in their net worth. I invested in 3-5 properties when the market was bleeding in 2008 and I told them, "I am buying a lot now. Are you joining me?" Ten of them jumped on the opportunity with me with no knowledge in real estate investments at all. I was able to share everything that they wanted to learn and even use the same people that worked for me. I did not ask for any return or payment from them, but my decision was coming from my heart, wanting to help others to better their finances.

They're now collecting their passive income in the range of 8-12% per year and each property has added for them in the hundreds of thousands. Believe me, there are still plenty of opportunity of investments out there. Make your commitment to learn about this business, have a plan, and you can succeed at it.

Time to Give Back

You've become a success and congratulations are in order. You are starting to live the dream. You have money that keeps on growing, and you have more free time than you thought you would, even though you have a large number of rental properties. What do you do now? While you will want to treat yourself on occasion, that's not the only thing that you should be doing.

There are others out there that are not as fortunate as you are. I'm a firm believer in giving to charity, as it really can make a difference in the world. You will feel better when you do as well. You can choose to give your time, or your money, or both. When you are in the position to give, please do. Make the world a better place. It will help you to find the true meaning of living. *I find giving and helping others gives me purpose to become more of myself so that I can help others more.*

CONCLUSION

In this chapter, I thought we'd have a few parting tips before we go, as well as reiterate some of the things that I feel are most important for you to take away from the book.

Growing the Business

As I've mentioned, you do not need to go into this business and buy up five properties all at once. In fact, that's probably a bad idea. What you do want to do, as we mentioned at the start, is to build your business slowly. Buy one property rental at first and come to grips with how everything works and what you need to do. This will allow you to keep your day job while you are learning, and then you will increase your number of rentals every year or so.

Making More Time

When you work a 9 to 5 job, it can often seem impossible to find more time in the day to work on your property rentals. I understand that it can be a big time investment, but you may have more time than you think throughout the day.

Consider your lunches and breaks. If you get two fifteen-minute breaks a day, as well as a half-hour lunch break, that's a full hour during the day that you could be working on your business. Now, you won't be able to get out and look at properties in person during that time, but you can get a substantial amount of your online research done. You could also use that time to make phone calls.

In addition, once you start to make some money from your first property rental and you are thinking about getting a second, consider cutting your hours at work if possible. Instead of working full-time, see if you could rework your schedule and go to part-time instead. Of course, this might not work with all jobs, and it is something that you would want to talk with your supervisors about in advance.

Something else that you might want to consider is working with a partner who can take care of some of the work for you. Working with a spouse is generally the best option, since you have the same goals in mind and it can be easier to make decisions since you are both on the same page (most of the time). Having someone else around to shoulder some of the work, whether it is research or getting a property ready to show to tenants, can make things much easier on you.

Getting and Staying Motivated

I also wanted to provide you with some tips for staying motivated on your journey. These tips will work quite well for getting into and staying in the property rental business. However, you will find that they can apply to everyday life as well.

- Set goals
- Break each goal down into achievable chunks
- Develop a strategy that will keep you on track
- Chart your milestones
- Get additional help and develop a support network that can provide you with a motivational boost (attend local real estate meetings)
- Celebrate the successes
- Think about the future financial freedom that awaits you

Always keeping the end goal in mind – your financial freedom – is easily the best motivator. It can help you to get through those early years while you are still at the 9 to 5, and it can spur you on to find more properties with great potential as you go. I worked at my mortgage company as long as I needed to accumulate more savings for the down payments and until my passive income exceed my goals. I did not have to trade my time for money since 2008.

2008-2011, I invested my time because I saw lifetime opportunity so I bought a lot more projects during these years.

Important Things to Remember

Here's a quick rundown of some of the most important things that you should remember from the book.

- *Analyze the properties you are considering buying – demographics, location, economic cycle, job growth, population growth, local industries, property condition and value, average price, the neighborhood, crime, property taxes, building permits, and whether natural disasters could cause an issue.*

- *Always invest in properties that will provide you with a positive cash flow, so you are making money each month rather than breaking even or, worse, losing money.*

- *Understand just how much cash flow you actually need for the property in order for it to be a success.*

- *You should invest in your hometown for your first rental property, or your first few rental properties. It's possible to invest and be successful in other cities and in other states, but it takes a bit more work.*

- *Understand what it takes to become a proper landlord and make sure you can meet the needs and the requests of your tenants.*

- *Determine whether you would be better off handling the landlord responsibilities on your own or by hiring a property management company instead.*

- *Find the right type of residential properties. Remember, single-family homes are going to be your best option, followed by townhouses, condos, and finally duplex, triplex, and fourplex properties.*

- *Find the purchase strategy that will work right for your current financial situation.*

- *Always hire a professional to inspect the property before you buy it.*

- *Create a thorough purchase contract.*

- *Increase your credit score, and manage it properly so that it keeps going up and stays high enough that you can get the best possible rates when you take out loans.*

- *Prepare for unexpected. Have a plan in place to help yourself minimize the damage from vacancies, maintenance costs, turnover, and evictions.*

- *Know when the best time to hold and the best time to sell is.*

- *Keep on building your financial future with property rentals.*

These bullet points are some of the biggest takeaways from the book. If you have questions, go back and reread those sections. Take things slow and familiarize yourself with the process of buying and renting out property one step at a time. You can do this.

You know what you want to accomplish. You have the tips and tools from this book to help guide you on your way. It's time that you took your first step toward achieving those dreams of financial freedom.

My Final Note: I Wish You the Best

Now that we have come to the end of the book, you should be in a much better position to understand just how and what you need to do in order to create wealth and passive income using cash flow rental properties that you buy and hold. There is a lot of information in the book, and I suggest that you keep it handy to review when you have questions, or just when you need a little extra motivation.

I am proof positive that this technique works as long as you are willing to put in the research and the time to make it work. **It's not a get-rich-quick scheme** – I don't believe in those. However, **it is a get-rich-smart plan that can serve you well now and for many years to come.**

I want you to be able to do the same things that I am doing and I want you to have the same success that I've found. **Now, it's time to start your journey to becoming a successful real estate investor and start creating wealth for yourself, so you can live the life of your dreams.**

"A journey of a thousand miles begins with a single step."
-- Lao Tzu

ABOUT THE AUTHOR

Korianne Mar is a bestselling author, seasoned RE investor, proud mom, and philanthropist. She was raised in Vietnam under a strict dad who sent her out of Vietnam in her late teens by herself, seeking freedom and opportunity called the American Dream. She came to America and worked non-stop to improve all aspects of her life, because she has a strong desire to live a well-balanced successful life with joy. She always reminds herself that she is a life-long learner. She worked two jobs to put herself though college and finished with a double major and no student debts.

After graduating from college, she landed an IT job at 3M, but her job was not challenging enough, so she left to find another opportunity that would keep her challenged. She landed another job with a high-tech startup, which offered her a 40% pay raise, but ten months after joining the company, it closed its doors because they ran out of money. Instead of getting another job, she refused to get back into the corporate world; though her experience, she knew that she would not enjoy working in a corporate job for another thirty years of her life, and missing out on a lot of interesting life experiences, but the biggest thing was *time* to spend with her kids and family. She knew that working for someone else would not provide her the freedom of time and financial independence that she desired.

Seeking out a new opportunity to become her own boss, she found a new opportunity in the finance sector, specializing in residential mortgages. She founded her own mortgage company after three months of extensive training with an experienced mortgage broker of thirty-five years. She closed over $150 million in residential mortgage loans. While running a very successful mortgage company, she also started building a rental business for her family, focusing on residential investments. She knows that one day if she and her husband are no longer able to work for any reason; there is a business that can support her family. By 2008, her real estate investments provided her financial independence, so she withdrew from the mortgage business.

Korianne started out buying just one rental property and then grew it into a rental portfolio of forty-five projects at one time. During the last fifteen years of her real estate career, she has bought/sold over ninety rental projects and had analyzed thousands of properties, but only selected the best one to add into her portfolio. She is now spending time managing rental projects in five different regions around the United States and is still actively selling/buying when an investment makes sense.

Korianne enjoys spending time with her family travelling around the world 3-4 times a year. She has been to forty-eight countries and would still love to do more. She is an avid fitness fanatic, loves outdoor activities, and is a consistent donor to humanity and homeless kids' projects in underdeveloped countries.

She lives in Texas with her family.

Connect with her at:
Her real estate investments blog: http://www.korianne.com
Linked In: https://www.linkedin.com/in/koriannemar
Instagram: http://www.instagram.com/koriannemar
Pineterest: http://www.pineterest.com/koriannemar

www.ingramcontent.com/pod-product-compliance
Lightning Source LLC
Chambersburg PA
CBHW070459200326
41519CB00013B/2645